AFTERSHOCKS
AND
OPPORTUNITIES

SCENARIOS FOR A POST-PANDEMIC FUTURE

Enjoy reading!

Warmly, Nell Watson

www.fastfuture.com

AFTERSHOCKS AND OPPORTUNITIES
SCENARIOS FOR A POST-PANDEMIC FUTURE

First published in United Kingdom by Fast Future Publishing in 2020

http://fastfuture.com

For information contact info@fastfuture.com

Paperback ISBN 978-1-9999311-6-2

eBook ISBN 978-1-9999311-5-5

Cover Designed by Dusan Arsenic

Original Cover Artwork by Vera Chernyshova via Pixabay.com

Cope Editing and Proof Reading by Steph Bennett, Proof Scrutiny

Interior design and typesetting by Consilience Media

Printed in the UK by the Print Trail

AFTERSHOCKS AND OPPORTUNITIES

SCENARIOS FOR A POST-PANDEMIC FUTURE

Edited by

Rohit Talwar
Steve Wells
Alexandra Whittington

www.fastfuture.com

About Fast Future

Fast Future is a research, insights, consulting, and executive education business. The company specializes in the use of foresight applied to explore the future of humanity, government and governance, the economy, business, key sectors, and exponentially advancing fields of science and technology. We have a particular interest in the impacts of developments such as artificial intelligence, robotics, exponential technologies, and disruptive thinking. We explore how they might impact life, society, nations, the planet, and the future of work, and the creation of the trillion-dollar sectors of the future.

Through speeches, webinars, studies, and books Fast Future explores, experiments with, and creates powerful future ideas and scenarios. The goal is to deliver critical insights to the individuals, governments, businesses, and agencies that want to consider and create a better future. Fast Future's books and newsletter provide insightful and thought provoking content and profile the latest thinking of established and emerging futurists, foresight researchers, and future thinkers from around the world.

Fast Future has a particular focus on ensuring these advances are harnessed to unleash individual potential and enable a very human future.

www.fastfuture.com
Twitter @fastfuture @futrbiz
www.facebook.com/FutrBiz
www.linkedin.com/company/fast-future-publishing

The Editors

Rohit Talwar is a global futurist, award-winning keynote speaker, author, and the CEO of Fast Future. His primary expertise lies in helping clients understand and shape the emerging future. He has a particular interest in how we can create a very human future by putting people at the center of the agenda. Rohit is the co-author of *Designing Your Future*. He is also co-author and editor of *The Future of Business; Beyond Genuine Stupidity—Ensuring AI Serves Humanity; The Future Reinvented—Reimagining Life, Society, and Business; A Very Human Future—Enriching Humanity in a Digitized World*; and *Opportunity at the Edge – Change, Challenge, and Transformation on the Path to 2025*.

rohit@fastfuture.com
Twitter @fastfuture
www.facebook.com/RohitKTalwar
www.linkedin.com/in/rohit-talwar-futurist-keynote-speaker

Steve Wells is a global futurist, keynote speaker, consultant with Fast Future, and the CEO of Informing Choices. He has a particular interest in helping clients anticipate and respond to the disruptive bursts of technological possibility that are shaping the emerging future. Steve is a contributor to and co-editor of *The Future of Business; Beyond Genuine Stupidity—Ensuring AI Serves Humanity; The Future Reinvented—Reimagining Life, Society, and Business; A Very Human Future—Enriching Humanity in a Digitized World*; and *Opportunity at the Edge – Change, Challenge, and Transformation on the Path to 2025*.

steve@fastfuture.com
Twitter @informingchoice
www.facebook.com/stevewells.futurist
www.linkedin.com/in/steve-wells-futurist-speaker

Alexandra Whittington is a futurist, writer, foresight director of Fast Future, and faculty member on the Futures program at the University of Houston. She has a particular expertise in future visioning and scenario planning. Alexandra is a contributor to *The Future of Business; Beyond Genuine Stupidity—Ensuring AI Serves Humanity; The Future Reinvented—Reimagining Life, Society, and Business; A Very Human Future—Enriching Humanity in a Digitized World;* and *Opportunity at the Edge – Change, Challenge, and Transformation on the Path to 2025.*

alex@fastfuture.com
Twitter @alexandra4casts
www.linkedin.com/in/alexandra-whittington-86794876

Contents

CONTENTS

Introduction

By Rohit Talwar, Steve Wells, and Alexandra Whittington

AFTERSHOCKS AND OPPORTUNITIES–SCENARIOS FOR A POST-PANDEMIC FUTURE

What different scenarios, challenges, and possibilities are taking shape for a post-pandemic world?

An Opportunity for Fresh Perspectives

While the world grapples with the current unfolding crisis, as futurists we know how important it is to also be thinking about the next horizon and beyond. This can help ensure that the decisions we make today do not simply lay the foundation for a new set of problems over the horizon. Equally, understanding the types of future that might emerge post-crisis can help us plan and prepare for those possibilities as we reshape our strategies today. Finally, such future insights might help us spot, train for, and adapt to the new opportunities, risks, and challenges that could arise as a post-pandemic world unfolds.

A Global Collaboration

In response to the need for future perspectives, Fast Future wanted to create this fast track book, which draws on the expertise, insight, ambition, and vision of 25 future thinkers from around the world. The goal is to provide individuals, leaders, and organizations with foresight, insight, challenge, visionary thinking, and navigational guidance on what lies ahead.

The initial call for contributions was issued on March 20th, 2020 and in total we received 115 incredibly diverse, insightful, provocative, and inspiring submissions from future thinkers across the planet. We have received more than enough really high-quality submissions to enable us to deliver a second, more thematically focused book, which is already in advanced stages of development. From the outset, the authors across both books have been incredibly supportive of the project and generous with their ideas.

Scenarios for a Post-Pandemic Future

The common goal of this group of writers is to provide provocations that will take the public discourse beyond the current debate. The aim is to acknowledge the importance of current priorities and also think about how we can create a safer and more sustainable world beyond reproduction numbers, testing strategies, personal protective equipment, lockdown policies, vaccination, and economic support. As many have said, a crisis is an ideal time to reset our thinking, refocus our strategies and policies, and try new ideas designed to lay the foundation for the next future and what comes after that. A future that the authors in this book believe can be fairer, more inclusive, more transparent, and more sustainable for all.

Four Core Themes

The concise, insightful, and action enabling ideas and provocations in this book are presented as an exploration of possible scenarios and development paths across four key domains that we believe should be of interest and extreme relevance to politicians, business leaders, civil society activities, and most importantly, the ordinary citizens of this planet:

Critical Shifts and Scenarios—exploring the developments taking place across every aspect of our collective thinking as a result of the pandemic experience.

Society and Social Policy—examining the implications and opportunities for the fabric and infrastructure of society as we look to tackle both the existing persistent challenges and the new ones that have arisen through the crisis. These frame an agenda for what could be developed in the future **new normal**.

Government and Economy—assessing how governments are, or should be, grappling with the challenges and consequences of balancing health and economic protection and recovery during and post-pandemic.

Business and Technology—outlining the possible implications, opportunities, and choices for business and our use of technology. Exploring how we might solve critical questions posed by the pandemic and lay the foundation for the future across health, education, social structures, commerce, and the design of our organizations.

CONTENTS
To help readers explore the many issues and opportunities on the post-pandemic global change agenda, the scene setting chapter and subsequent four sections of the book cover the following topics:

Scenarios for a Post-Pandemic World
Rohit Talwar (Global Futurist and CEO), Steve Wells (Global Futurist and Foresight Consultant), and Alexandra Whittington (Global Futurist and Foresight Director), Fast Future, UK/US
This chapter lays out the spectrum of possibilities of how key drivers of change may play out including the economic recovery, evolution of the pandemic, health, political, consumer sentiment, business, socio-demographic, science and technology, and environment. Four scenarios are then presented exploring how these drivers might come together over time.

PART 1: CRITICAL SHIFTS AND SCENARIOS

Navigating a New Landscape
Rohit Talwar, Steve Wells, and Alexandra Whittington, Fast Future
This chapter presents a horizon scan of eight powerful shifts taking place for governments, society, individuals, businesses, and markets. When viewed collectively, these shifts could reshape literally every aspect of life as we understand it on this planet.

A New Planetary Narrative
Sohail Inayatullah is the UNESCO Chair in Futures Studies at USIM, Malaysia, professor at Tamkang University, Taiwan, and a researcher at global think-tank Metafuture.org., Australia
Six paradigms or discourses are used to understand possible responses to the current pandemic. These are: disease and cure, the next disease, beyond meat, leadership and climate change, the end of capitalism, and a final discourse that suggests we may be able to create a new Renaissance.

A Laboratory for the Future
Liselotte Lyngsø is a futurist and managing partner of Future Navigator, Denmark
The pandemic has thrown us into pitch black water, amplifying trends that were already emerging. Families have had to adapt to spending time together in a whole new way. Workplaces have learned to work together—apart. New rules apply. The planet has effectively become a future laboratory with an amazing opportunity to kick-start our experimentation for the world of tomorrow.

World War Contagion—Strategies in the Fight Against Our Common Enemy
Miranda Mantey is an experienced researcher, foresight practitioner, and strategist at ATB Financial in Calgary, Canada
What does the world become when the greatest war in recent history is not with an enemy state, but with a pandemic? This chapter is an

exploration of the social, political, and technological implications of a future where the biggest enemy could be living inside of each and every one of us.

Five Ways Our Post-Lockdown World Could Change for the Better

Sheila Moorcroft is a futurist and director of Realising Your Future, UK
This chapter explores how actions and attitudes developed during the crisis could change our post-pandemic world. Sheila argues that it will be more remote, but more local and that organizations will be under greater scrutiny to do right by all stakeholders. She explores how public gratitude to essential workers could realign politics and attitudes to tax policy.

The Pandemic and the Medical Enlightenment—The View from 2035

Jerry Edling is a broadcaster, editor, and writer for KNX in Los Angeles, US
The public policy responses to the pandemic were, in some cases, haphazard; but the resolve of people around the world was stalwart. Little did anybody know that the battle against it would trigger a quantum leap forward in healthcare and create a new paradigm for the world economy. Looking back from the year 2035, this chapter asks, how did the pandemic revolutionize medicine and transform the way the world is connected?

Does the Proverbial Cloud Created by the Pandemic of 2020 Have a Silver Lining?

Paul Plant is an independent strategy and transformation consultant and chief listening officer of Radicle Consulting, UK
A pragmatic yet upbeat prognosis of the possible consequences of the most momentous global event of the Internet era. This chapter considers the likely differences that people foresee in the post-pandemic world. These are looked at in terms of what we might appreciate more, the silver lining to the pandemic's dark cloud, and a few things that might never be the same again.

The Case for New Progressive, Socially Focused Economic Initiatives

Dr Bruce Lloyd, emeritus professor of Strategic Management at London South Bank University, UK

"Never waste a good crisis," is the mantra of this chapter in which the author explores the opportunity for new initiatives, and the need to accelerate existing ones. The goal, Bruce argues, is to advance socially focused economic agendas for countries around the globe.

PART 2: SOCIETY AND SOCIAL POLICY

Retroshock—A Return to Roots

Eleanor "Nell" Watson is a tech ethicist, machine learning researcher, social reformer, and a member of the AI Faculty at Singularity University, Belgium

This chapter explores the potential for a radical, more human and planet centric path to the future. Our global civilization has never come so close to systemic collapse as in the year 2020. But like a forest fire, having scorched away the incumbent chaff of a complacent civilization, the willowy seeds of a new culture had fertile space in which to grow.

Policing the New Normal

Katherine Van Gurp (Chief Executive Officer) and Mike Richmond (Strategic Foresight Advisor), the Australia New Zealand Policing Advisory Agency

Globally, police have been catapulted into unfamiliar public health roles. In Australia and New Zealand, as elsewhere, police have mobilized rapidly to meet this challenge and manage the risks to their workforces' wellbeing, at the same time as cascading impacts have altered the criminal landscape. This chapter explores the forces that could shape the new normal of policing in the post-pandemic world.

This IS a Drill–Preparing for the Next Pandemic

Morgan D. Kauffman is a futurist, systems modeler, and data scientist, US
Pandemics are disruptive by their nature, with impacts ranging from the loss of life and disruption of mental health to the economic consequences of sudden lockdowns and periods of quarantine. This chapter asks what if we tried to lessen that disruption by building preparations into our lives through bi-yearly "**Quarantine Month**" drills that could save lives and soften the blow of the next pandemic.

Preparing for a New Way of Being

Julia Paulette Hollenbery is a therapist, teacher, and author, UK
This chapter is a philosophical evocation of a radically different and unpredictable future. What will enable us to navigate the new landscape well? We will need a spiritual shift in our way of life. We will need to develop a new "operating system" based on body and heart, as well as mind.

Zoomers Learning About Their Roots in History Class

Sylvia Gallusser is a futurist and researcher studying health, aging, work, learning, and transhumanism at Silicon Humanism, US
Fifteen years after the pandemic, a history teacher revisits the aftermath of the crisis with her students, who happen to be the first generation of youth from the baby boom that ensued. Beyond the medical, economic, and social impact of the pandemic, the wounds turn out to be more acute, profound, and intimate than anticipated.

When the Future was Bright

Joe Tankersley is a futurist, author, and former leader of Walt Disney Imagineering's foresight group, US
The pandemic has inspired a wide range of future scenarios, many of them painting optimistic pictures of a post-pandemic world. But, what if they discount the power of social conditioning and the barriers to change? This chapter explores what might happen if we prematurely declare victory against the pandemic and rush to return to "normal."

Post-Pandemic Homes

Alexandra Whittington is a global futurist, speaker, writer, and foresight director at Fast Future, and an adjunct lecturer at the University of Houston, US

With social distancing and isolation measures introduced to limit the spread of the virus, this chapter explores the longer-lasting impact of how life in the home might change through the use of technology and behavior. Asking, will future homes become a protective haven of safety and wellbeing?

PART 3: GOVERNMENT AND ECONOMY

Post-Pandemic Government—A Futurist Perspective

Rohit Talwar, Steve Wells, and Alexandra Whittington, Fast Future

Since the 1960s futurists have advised on both emerging and persistent risks and response strategies to mitigate the impacts and aftereffects. So, what lessons can we learn from the past and apply to both our current pandemic responses and our future scenarios? This chapter explores ten principles to be factored in by governments, businesses, and civil society.

More Aware, More Agile, More Alive

David W. Wood is a futurist, chair of London Futurists, and principal of Delta Wisdom, UK

This chapter discusses how, following the wake-up of the pandemic, a new world is not only possible but highly desirable—a world that is more aware, more agile, and more alive. Whether this kind of transition takes place over the coming years will determine if the longer-term future for humanity is dismal or glorious.

Using the Crisis to Remake Government for the Future

Geoff Mulgan is professor of Collective Intelligence, Public Policy, and Social Innovation at University College London, UK

The pandemic could be just a one-off blip, with normal service resuming once the worst of it is over. But it could be used to accelerate changes that were long overdue. This chapter looks at how governments around the world have coped with the crisis and how their actions may point to radically different approaches in the future, from data to mental health, and civic mobilization to transparency.

The Great Separation
Bronwyn Williams is a futurist, economist, trend analyst, and partner at Flux Trends and Apollo42, South Africa
The pandemic is by no means an equalizing crisis. Indeed, one of the most significant lasting socio-economic effects of the crisis will be the opening up of the fault lines running underneath fragile modern society. The center may not hold.

Which Way America? Four Alternative Futures
Leland Shupp is a foresight and design led company growth strategist and principal at Lee Shupp Consulting, US
The US plays a pivotal role in the global economy and in international institutions, but the future of the US is highly uncertain, depending on the shape of the economic recovery and the outcome of the coming election. This chapter explores four alternative futures that are possible over the next 3-5 years.

Reshaping the Economic Agenda
Rohit Talwar, Steve Wells, and Alexandra Whittington, Fast Future
Many countries are wrestling with how to balance an immense agenda of short-term priorities against the need to ensure a path to a sustainable and viable medium- to long-term future. This chapter examines five critical economic policy areas in which robust, bold, and innovative thinking will be required to map a path forward on societal grand challenges.

PART 4: BUSINESS AND TECHNOLOGY

Snapback—Don't Expect a Post-Pandemic Remote Working Boom

Tom Cheesewright is an applied futurist working with governments and global Fortune 500 companies, UK

Remote working has many documented advantages for both employer and employee. With the lockdown enforcing remote working for many, the expectation has been for a larger uptake in a post-lockdown world. This chapter argues that such predictions ignore the very real personal and cultural barriers to adoption that remain.

Transformative Re-Structuring

Alida Draudt is a foresight strategist, strategy director at AKQA, and an adjunct professor at California College of the Arts, US

This chapter explores the application of Transformative Re-Structuring, using the Alternative Futures foresight model, to look at how post-pandemic life and business could transform to embrace new operations, behaviors, and beliefs that impact all aspects of society in 2023.

Navigating the Post-Pandemic Economy—Doing Business at the Speed of Change

Rob Caldera is a strategic foresight and change practitioner and the owner and managing principal of Future|Shift Consulting, US

Already reeling from today's exponential pace of change, the pandemic has made it starkly clear that today's businesses were not built to handle sudden, disruptive events. This chapter presents a scenario exploring how the pandemic could accelerate the future of work, as companies rebuild themselves into change-ready organizations.

The Rise of Personal Digital Twins

Roberto Saracco is a freelance consultant, writer on technology innovation, and co-chair of the IEEE Digital Reality Initiative, US

Based on the work done at the IEEE Future Direction Committee in the Digital Reality Initiative this thought-provoking scenario describes the use of personal digital twins with specific reference to epidemic detection and management. Roberto explores how personal digital twins could become a seamless extension of our body and an augmentation of the human species.

The Next Futures of Organizations, Work, and the Workplace

Rohit Talwar, Steve Wells, and Alexandra Whittington, Fast Future
The pandemic has had a remarkably rapid impact on organizational activity and behavior, and we are already beginning to develop insights on the emerging possible futures of business, work, and the workplace. This chapter discusses ten shifts that organizations are having to embrace that could have lasting impacts.

CONCLUSION

The Change Agenda for a Post-Pandemic World

Rohit Talwar, Steve Wells, and Alexandra Whittington, Fast Future
The crisis has surfaced individual, societal, national, and international fragilities. Our challenge is to respond by building a post-pandemic world that is fair, open, inclusive, sustainable, and rich in opportunities for all. This chapter outlines ten key themes that could help frame the resulting recovery agenda at national and global level.

Scenarios for a Post-Pandemic World

By Rohit Talwar, Steve Wells, and Alexandra Whittington

What scenarios could play out as we navigate through lockdown and then into a post-pandemic era?

It seems reasonable to start a book exploring what the near- to medium-term future might hold by laying out some possible scenarios for a post-pandemic world. We have used a standard two by two matrix, **driving force model** of scenario construction. Our two core driving forces making up the axes are The Evolution of the Pandemic and The Shape of Economic Recovery—giving us four possible scenarios:

1. The Long Goodbye (poorly contained pandemic, deep and prolonged downturn)
2. The VIP Economy (poorly contained pandemic, vibrant economic rebound)
3. Safe but Hungry (eradication of the pandemic, deep and prolonged downturn)
4. Inclusive Abundance (eradication of the pandemic, vibrant economic rebound).

We have then factored in what might be happening to a range of other key driving forces—namely health, political, business, consumer sentiment, socio-demographic, science and technology, and environment.

The table below represents the range of possible outcomes for each force. The resulting four scenarios are then expanded upon.

Factor	Outcome Range	
Shape of Economic Recovery	*Deep and prolonged downturn* US GDP falls 20% in 2020, other leading nations decline 10-30%. National priorities dominate, little global coordination, trade tensions, country failures. Concerted global action in mid- to late-2021 starts to drive a turnaround.	*Vibrant economic rebound* Banks globally commit to low interest lending-led recovery, driving a V-shaped bounce back. Coordinated recovery led by G7, G20, EU, ASEAN, SCO, GCC, and the African Union. Focus on globally inclusive recovery. New experiments around economic and financial models emerge by late 2022.
Evolution of the Pandemic	*Poorly contained pandemic* Many Asian/European nations end lockdown and suppress a second peak. US and UK have multiple peaks and worst developed nation levels of infection and deaths. Pandemic at uncontrollable levels in developing countries—India, Pakistan, Brazil, Afghanistan, Syria, and Yemen among the worst affected.	*Eradication of the pandemic* Coordinated global effort to establish effective health testing, treatment, and vaccination capabilities worldwide from July 2020 onwards. Global health infrastructure, capacity, skills, and delivery systems prioritized by UN, WHO, G7, and G20. Strong multinational CSR focus on enhancing local healthcare.
Viral Spread	Over 10M cases and 3M deaths globally by the end of 2020. 2021 cases and deaths continue rising in poorer nations	2020 global infection rates peak at 6M cases and 600K deaths. 2021 sees global infection rates fall sharply
Virus Testing	Less than 20% get antigen testing globally by 12/2020. Less than 10% get antibody testing globally by 12/2020.	Over 50% get antigen testing globally by 12/2020. Over 25% get antibody testing globally by 12/2020.

Vaccination	First proven vaccines not available until 01/2022. Less than 25% vaccinated globally by 01/2023.	First proven vaccines available by 01/2021. Over 50% vaccinated globally by 12/2021.
Global GDP 2020 Growth	-6%	-3%
Global GDP 2021 Growth	-2%	4-6%
Global GDP 2022 Growth	0-2%	4-6%
Political	Rising nationalism, citizen unrest and high government distrust in many nations, several governments displaced, sporadic peaks in domestic riots and civil wars, global institutions increasingly sidelined.	Confidence builds as second peaks avoided and economies rebound. Emergency powers repealed quickly. Increasing experimentation with citizen engagement and more inclusive governance models. Modernization of global institutions.
Business	Extreme caution as lockdowns lift. Investment and business confidence continue to decline as second and third waves of closures and redundancies hit. Recession drives down 2021 revenue targets and budgets, and the impacts roll into 2022.	Continued government stimulus, bank loan support to businesses, and pent-up demand drive business spending. Investment in automation and AI seen as a priority. Strong focus on driving digital literacy, reskilling, developing new sectors and businesses, and increased virtual working.
Consumer Sentiment	Post-lockdown spending peak masks broader house-hold financial concerns. Focus on self-preservation and financial survival.	Optimism returns quickly as lockdowns lift. Rapid growth drives job creation and communal feel-good factor. Strong focus on improving provision for the most marginalised and least well served in society.

Socio-demo-graphic	Deep erosion of trust in many countries. Persistent and growing unemployment deepens divides. Mental health problems and domestic violence cases reach peak levels. Outward migration from failing nations spark new refugee crises.	Trust is the new currency. Community spirit developed during lockdown helps drive nations forward. Populations show increasing concern for those highlighted as suffering the most socially and economically. Cross-societal commitment to enhancing health, elder care, and education.
Science and Technology (S&T)	Faith in science and experts erodes quickly as recriminations start over the way the crisis was handled. Deep split between those individuals and businesses with the resources to invest in advanced technologies and those who can't afford them.	A cornerstone of growth and recovery plans is accelerated investment in key S&T fields that can drive industry transformation and enable new sectors. Global R&D collaborations formed in the pandemic spawn new alliances and process innovation.
Environment	Some of the improvements on emissions, water quality, and air pollution sustain due to lower levels of economic activity. Generally, goals for environmental improvement are sidelined in pursuit of economic recovery at all costs.	Corporate bailouts increasingly tied to delivering on the SDGs and environmental targets. Post-pandemic consumers place increasing focus on buying from firms with strong ethical and environmental credentials across their supply chains.

The Long Goodbye (poorly contained pandemic, deep and prolonged downturn)

This scenario sees the beginning of a slow and painful end to the systems, structures, and hierarchies that are no longer fit for purpose in a highly interconnected and interdependent world. The deep health and economic malaise see the worst affected developing nations in particular yoyo in and out of lockdown. Lacking the resources to scale up testing and treatment, they have few policy tools at their disposal. The US fails to control the situation effectively and sees continued growth of infections and death rates into the summer of 2020, with a very slow decline and periodic second and third peaks across the country. This hampers both the domestic recovery and global trade—with nations fearful of opening their borders to US visitors.

An inwardly focused world takes a long time to acknowledge that this global problem requires a global solution and a reworking of mechanisms from health to trade, financial markets, and local governance—particularly in developing economies. In mid- to late-2021 a coalition of global institutions, businesses, billionaire philanthropists, and visionary social change agents reach agreement on a new recovery plan for the planet. Buy-in is secured slowly as the leaders of those countries in the most need of help prove reluctant to give up power in favor of progress. Ultimately a five-year program of economic, social, environmental, and governmental developments are agreed with richer nations acting as coach, mentor, and sponsor to those in the most need of help and reform.

The VIP Economy (poorly contained pandemic, vibrant economic rebound)

This scenario sees an exacerbation of the already existent divides within and between countries. While the global picture is bleak, those with reasonable incomes and wealth can effectively ensure they are first in line for antigen and antibody testing and vaccinations when they arrive. Strong social distancing measures are put in place within many countries to protect the middle class and wealthy from those in poorer, more densely populated areas with a higher propensity to infection. This allows parts of the economy to relaunch quickly, with investment bargain hunters picking up the distressed assets of failed businesses at knock-down prices.

Governments in developed economies emphasize the need to reboot economies and prioritize the protection and healthcare of investors, financiers, business owners, managers, and employees of the enterprises most likely to drive economic recovery. Travel bans are imposed on the worst affected nations, while others face enforced quarantine on arrival. In the developing world, many governments effectively write off segments of the population as irrecoverable, cordon them off from the rest of society, and leave nature to take its course.

Safe but Hungry (eradication of the pandemic, deep and prolonged downturn)

In this scenario, a large number of economies experience multiple infection waves and respond to public pressure to prioritize health over economy. Government resources are directed at rapid rollout of testing, treatment, and vaccination programs in search of permanent protection against the virus. Lockdown orders are lifted very slowly and the most stringent of social distancing controls and protective measures are imposed on businesses and public transport. Bars, restaurants, theaters, cinemas, and hotels face such restrictive measures in many locations that they choose not to reopen or repurpose themselves.

The resulting economic recovery is much slower to materialize but ultimately feels more sustainable and inclusive because of the increased confidence that the virus is under greater control. The picture varies across the globe, with near normal levels of business and social activity taking place in those nations that got control of the situation and effectively eradicated the virus early.

Inclusive Abundance (eradication of the pandemic, vibrant economic rebound)

This scenario depicts a world where those in power accept that this is an opportunity to innovate and transform in response to the pandemic. Alongside an accelerated pursuit of mass testing, treatment, and vaccination, a globally inclusive regeneration around the Sustainable Development goals (SDGs) becomes the chosen way forward as the true economic scale of the crisis becomes apparent. Alongside regenerative investment in new sectors, skills, and green new deal policies, governments also look to work in partnership to address the challenges of the weakest nations.

Science and technology are seen as central to the new agenda with a focus on ensuring that every nation has local capabilities in fields as diverse as vertical farming, synthetic biology, small footprint manufacturing (e.g. pharmaceuticals, vaccines, consumer goods), and artificial intelligence (AI) as a means of increasing resilience against future pandemics. The reform of education and learning at every level is prioritized to ensure that adults and children alike are acquiring the tools they need for an uncertain future—from sector specific training and social capabilities, through to the mindset and transferable skills such as problem solving, accelerated learning, and collaboration required to move easily from job to job.

Mechanisms such as universal basic incomes and services are used as a temporary measure to support those in need while they transition and learn key skills to enable them to find or create new employment opportunities. This is by no means a perfect world and many long-standing challenges persist. The SDGs have not been fully delivered, but a more inclusive future focused agenda has been embraced by many and the benefits are beginning to show through.

Conclusion

Scenarios, by their nature, are meant to present extreme possibilities that force us to think differently about alternative paths to the future. The four scenarios here are designed to challenge, stimulate, inspire, and provoke in equal measure and prepare the intellectual landscape across which a range of ideas will now be explored across the chapters of this book.

- *From where we stand today, what are the most positive post-pandemic scenarios we can envisage?*
- *Can we create a truly abundant and inclusive future for all, or do we have to accept that there will always be those who global society choose to leave behind?*
- *How might the power brokers on the planet be brought together to align around a scenario of truly inclusive global post-pandemic development?*

CRITICAL SHIFTS AND SCENARIOS

Navigating a New Landscape

By Rohit Talwar, Steve Wells, and Alexandra Whittington

What reasonable assumptions can we make about the kinds of global post-pandemic shifts that could take place for governments, society, individuals, businesses, and markets over the next few years?

Now that the pandemic has spread across the entire planet, there is a growing understanding that the economic and social ramifications could last far longer than the virus itself. In this chapter, we present a horizon scan of eight powerful shifts that are beginning to take form and which, taken collectively, will reshape literally every aspect of life as we understand it on this planet.

1. Restoring the Old Order vs. Total System Reboot

The debate is raging about how we use the "gift of a crisis" to determine the right political, economic, societal, and global governance structures to help us navigate the immediate aftermath and lay the foundations for the next ten years. We appreciate that there are now many voices suggesting that this crisis should trigger a reboot of the global economy, the entire model of capitalism, and civil society infrastructure. The aim being to create a sustainable economic and social architecture for the digital age.

Others are arguing that with so much chaos on so many fronts, we should go back to the pre-pandemic models we understand and then adjust those as the situation plays out. Their case is that already overwhelmed societies simply do not have the intellectual or emotional energy to embrace radical new ideas. These ideas encompass green new deals, alternative models for capitalism, higher taxes, increased citizen engagement in decision-making, universal basic incomes (UBI), an enlarged welfare state, new governance institutions, revamped voting systems, and greater state ownership of businesses.

So how do make our choices? Many of the challenges, ideas, and visions presented across the pages of this book suggest that there is no going back. The authors argue that the old models have run their course. The suggestion is to embed wide-scale innovation and experimentation in the design of what comes next in the pursuit of a new normal—albeit a potentially turbulent one. While we see the desire to return to the old and familiar, the reality is that many of these systems were already under strain.

The pandemic has offered a range of insights into the possibilities for change from a more respectful relationship with the planet to a deeper embrace of working from home and creative approaches to online learning. Multiple shifts are taking place, many unplanned and enforced. The biggest shift here could be the one in the mindsets of government, civil society, business, and citizens to accept the need for real change. The question is whether these groups will welcome more exploratory and experimental approaches to finding the right next steps to take us towards a fairer, more transparent, sustainable, inclusive, and positive future.

2. For the Love of Facts

The crisis has put society on a rapid learning curve, encompassing everything from the nature of viral transmission and reproduction rates, to the different ways in which countries interpret terms such as infection, death, and recovery in the context of the virus. It has taught many of us to become more discerning about the source and reliability of the information we are receiving. Governments are being challenged to share and explain the scientific advice they are getting and acting upon. Global comparison charts now place every nation's strategy under the spotlight. Pointed questions are being asked about response strategies in comparison with China's neighbors such as Hong Kong and Taiwan, which have attributed only four and seven deaths respectively to the pandemic. In contrast, those much further away like the UK and US are reporting over 35,000 and 90,000 deaths respectively as we go to press.

Now that society has learned the value of trustworthy information sources, it is unlikely that we will give up our newfound love of reliable data. Nor does it seem likely that we will relax our quest for greater scientific knowledge, or our desire to understand the thought processes that translate scientific advice and opinion into government policy. These shifts are evident around the world and are driving people to create parallel knowledge-sharing networks, alternative scientific advisory panels, and mechanisms for genuine dialog and consensus building across populations. Such mechanisms could become powerful forces in validating the information we receive and in pressuring governments for greater transparency and engagement.

3. Government Response Mechanisms

At each stage of the pandemic's evolution in different countries, we have seen dramatic variation in government responses. This is particularly true in relation to issues such as social isolation to try and flatten and delay the peak of infection and how lockdown or stay at home orders might be relaxed. We have also seen some governments admit that the emerging evidence has led to policy changes in relation to delay, deterrence, containment, and recovery strategies. Others have been less transparent.

In many cases, the variation in responses has been attributable to the relative preparedness for a large-scale domestic health-related disruption. However well or poorly countries had prepared, we can anticipate a future where the public demands far greater emergency readiness. This would include the response mechanisms to mobilize people and resources, and to provide financial support to individuals and organizations. Equally, we can expect governments and their key officials to be better trained in anticipating and acting early on each phase of a crisis as it unfolds. In practical terms this could range from having localized supply agreements for critical medical equipment, through to always being seen to be aware of and preparing for a range of possibilities of "what could happen after what happens next."

4. The Global Economy

The prospect of national recessions in multiple large economies has now been baked in by many financial analysts and stock markets. This is also driving the prospect of a global downturn or even a depression. Economists, central banks, and the financial markets are debating the nature and duration of the path to recovery, with talk of V, U, W, L, and inverted square root all being offered as possible shapes for the path out of the crisis. The reality is that no one really knows, because the post-lockdown impacts on different sectors is hard to gage.

Some suggest that we could witness an initial euphoric peak followed by a rapid decline again in sectors such as automotive, which have seen a 90% or more decrease in sales during the crisis. Others, such as aviation and hotels, are already planning on the assumption of lower long-term expectations and a slower recovery, which is driving widespread redundancies across both sectors. The direct and knock-on effects of sector turbulence and potential redundancies, coupled with a potentially accelerated pace of job automation, are proving almost impossible to factor into economic models.

As industries reshape their supply chains and geographic footprints, the impact on major economies such as China and the US are also the subject of much conjecture. For example, there is a real prospect of firms reducing their reliance on China as a production hub and moving to establish more local facilities in many key markets. This might help drive investment and increase business resilience.

From a global systems perspective, in the global financial crisis (GFC) of 2007-08, major nations worked together to stabilize the world's economy and prevent total meltdown. At present, there seems less willingness to pursue coordinated action. However, with the scale of devastation threatening to be far deeper and more widespread, and the cost of recovery far higher, the shift to a more coordinated and globally inclusive recovery plan is becoming an imperative.

Part of any coordinated recovery strategy—particularly for the most economically unstable economies—will need to include building sustainable foundations for the future. This could encompass investment in and development of new sectors, learning and skills, digital literacy, adoption of greener solutions across the economy, bolstering of key institutions, and capacity building across government and civil society.

5. Financial Markets

Many stock markets have been in freefall and fluctuating quite dramatically. Inevitably, bargain hunters have periodically stepped back in because they think prices have fallen below critical levels and believe that this is a good time to buy. Clearly markets are spooked, with the Financial Times FT100 index recording its second highest percentage fall in history and the US Dow Jones Industrial Average seeing both its biggest daily fall in history and largest one day gain since the 2007-08 GFC.

Market volatility is driven by a combination of factors. Firstly, there are genuine concerns about the outlook for particular businesses. For example, hotels and airlines are among the sectors most heavily impacted by the virus, by the travel controls imposed by different nations, and by customer safety concerns. Secondly, there is the concern about human behavior – with caution driving down consumption, boosting the level of personal savings, and increasing the potential for market collapse—triggering a pre-emptive wave of panic selling.

In some cases, shareholders are being forced to sell, even on market downswings, in order to meet their ongoing commitments such as pension payments and life insurance policy maturities. The final factor driving volatility is a desire for safe havens, leading many large institutional investors such as pension funds to sell shareholdings and buy into hopefully more secure government debt—effectively at negative interest rates. The hope is that this will at least preserve the bulk of their investment. Those willing to stay in for the long term may not see losses realized if the markets recover relatively quickly.

Alternatively, they could see a massive write down in their portfolio valuations—exacerbated by the failure of companies tipped over the edge by the crisis.

Those sitting on large pools of uninvested funds could be the biggest beneficiaries—coming back into markets when they finally turn a corner. Stock market fluctuations, the disruption of economies, and the level of confidence in national governments will also drive behavior in foreign exchange markets. Some are arguing that this could be the start of far larger contagion that could dwarf the impacts of the 2008 Global Financial Crises.

6. General Business Responses

Businesses have increasingly been erring on the side of caution and are likely to become even more risk averse if trading conditions do not improve quickly following the lifting of restrictions. There are concerns that, once the financial support dries up, we may see further waves of redundancies and firm closures among businesses relying on government furlough schemes to keep their workforce employed. Hence, the full impact on redundancies, business failures, and debt defaults are only likely to become clear once economies have had a few months of trading with fewer social distancing controls. Some are already suggesting that Italy's recovery from this could take five years or more.

Elsewhere, we can expect a continuation of working practices and spending constraints put in place when lockdowns began. These include encouraging staff to continue working from home or smaller remote sites to prevent the risk of infection and reduce office over-heads. With the success of video communication, non-essential travel for meetings, internal events, and attendance at external events could continue to be banned or strongly discouraged—irrespective of what government policy is.

Cost control will become an increasingly prime directive in the face of declining demand. However, some may also see the need to think about the longer term, deepen and retain customer relationships, and take the opportunity to manage their organization in a slightly more foresighted, and less frantic and breathless manner. Hence, measures we can expect to see emerging would include investing more in customer service training to differentiate themselves and retain customer loyalty, and in digital literacy to increase efficiency and flexibility.

Strategically, this may be seen as an opportunity to train leaders and managers in how to use foresight, horizon scanning, and scenario planning to develop anticipatory and forward-thinking capabilities. We can also expect a continued increase in the adoption of online training solutions, collective intelligence tools, and group decision-making systems that has already been evidenced.

Many may see this as an opportunity to pause for reflection, leading to the prioritization and cancellation or suspension of current business initiatives to focus on the vital few. Many will be accelerating the testing of the capacity of systems to support large numbers of staff working from home and remote locations on a long-term basis.

Widespread cost-cutting measures on non-essential spending could be increasingly commonplace—alongside reducing revenue forecasts and budgets for the next financial year. The virus could also see a growing number of firms investing in automation to reduce their dependency on a human workforce and lower their cost base. Hence, Robotic Process Automation and hyperautomation could become major priorities. Alongside this we can anticipate increasing use of on-demand outsourcing to reduce fixed staffing costs.

Some may look to lead by example and go as far as making longer-term cuts to top leadership and middle management remuneration packages and suspending bonuses until performance rebounds. Those worse affected may also be asking staff to take longer-term voluntary pay cuts and encouraging them to take unpaid leave until trading conditions improve. Others may look to renegotiate the terms of contracts, leases, loans, and mortgages—with a particular emphasis on cancellation charges. While many firms will be delaying major investment projects, others may see an opportunity to accelerate major investment projects, taking advantage of the willingness of desperate vendors to cut prices to secure sales.

7. Supply Chains and Business Footprint

There was clearly some sourcing disruption as a result of large-scale factory closures in China in January and February. Many of these supply chains are back in operation now. However, it is as yet unclear what the long-term impact might be on the ability of firms to source critical raw materials resulting from widespread infection and forced quarantine in many countries. Concerns over continuity of supply and price volatility is already driving firms and governments to source more locally. The crisis is also driving a number of firms to re-evaluate the operational risk and the economics of their geographic manufacturing and distribution footprint.

Many may consider that, with the extent to which production is now automated, they can bring production either back to their home markets or distribute it even more widely. We could see a growth in much smaller footprint facilities across a number of markets, with a view to hopefully minimizing global disruption and maximizing the capacity to service all of the current markets that businesses are in and those that could be important for the future. The crisis could also drive innovation in newer approaches such as vertical farming, containerized farming, and 3D printing.

8. Critical Sector Disruption—Air Transport

Air transport is the center of the global economy and most nations' trading ambitions. For example, increased trade with nations across the planet beyond the EU is the central economic pillar of the **"Global Britain"** post-Brexit strategy. This is also currently looking like the sector that could experience the most immediate and severe impacts. We have seen a near total shutdown of global travel with flight volumes down over 80%, many airlines completely grounded, and others making redundancies and seeking government bailouts.

The industry is currently talking about a two- to three-year recovery period, with a new normal of 80% of 2019 revenues and flight activity by 2023. The International Air Transport Association (IATA) is predicting a US$314 billion loss in global passenger revenues by the airlines for 2020—a 48% decline on 2019. Airport Council

International (ACI) is projecting a worldwide loss in airport revenues of US$76 billion for 2020—a decline of 45% against the forecast for the year.

How the industry recovers, and its long-term state of health, are likely to have a significant direct impact on the shape and speed of global economic recovery. Aviation sector recovery will depend on its capacity to win back passenger confidence and continue innovating, the cost of new safety measures, the impact of corporate travel restrictions, rationalization expenses, and the loss of revenues on routes that are deemed unprofitable. With the potential for the closure of certain routes and airport closures, some locations could see an even bigger negative economic impact.

This list represents just a small fraction of the range of shifts taking place as a result of the pandemic. Many more are covered on the following pages. Taken collectively, we see a rapidly unfolding situation, with deep uncertainty about what happens next, and many thrown into chaos by a lack of foresight and preparedness. The challenge now is to ensure that these ideas and those of the other authors in this book will act as a stimulus for more radical and wide-ranging recovery plans that provide hope for all sections of global society.

- *How often do you undertake horizon scanning and scenario thinking exercises to identify and explore critical emerging shifts, and how do they feed into strategy development and operational planning?*
- *How do you go about training managers and leaders to think about the future and factor in possible shifts and developments that are not on their current radar?*
- *How well prepared do you feel to share with your teams about the emerging shifts you are seeing and the level of uncertainty you are experiencing?*

A New Planetary Narrative

By Sohail Inayatullah

What narratives can we use to make sense of the changing world in light of the pandemic and its consequences?

During the global financial crisis over a decade ago, the Financial Times[1] reported that at its heart this was a narrative crisis. How you dealt with it depended on the story you used. Was it a mortgage crisis, a banking crisis, a geopolitical crisis of the shift to the Pacific (higher savings rates), a financial crisis, or even a crisis of capitalism? Ultimately, a deeper potential crisis was avoided, and Wall Street was saved at the expense of Main Street. China also helped to save the day and the world returned to relative normalcy. The window for a possibility of deep change did not materialize.

We are in a similar situation today. As during the French Revolution, time is plastic, we have entered uncharted waters. Once the crisis nears its end, many will be tempted to go back to the world we knew. However, this is also the opportunity to create a different world—a portal, as author and activist Arundhati Roy argues.[2] As biosecurity expert Peter Black argues, "Historically, pandemics have forced humans to break with the past and imagine their world anew. This one is no different. It is a portal, a gateway between one world and the next."[3]

What we do will be decided by the narrative we use. How deep do we wish to go, how much do we wish to change? Here I present six paradigms, or discourses, to understand the possible responses to the current crisis.

Disease and Cure

If this is merely a disease crisis, then the answer is easy: find the cure and the vaccine. Ensure open science, the free-flow information, and find the medical solutions. The main insights will be that the global science community—empowered by the free flow of information—working together can create the difference. As a Spanish biological researcher commented: "You give the footballer one million euros a month and biological researcher 1,800 euros. You are looking for a treatment now. Go to Cristiano Ronaldo or Messi now and they will find you a cure."[4] Science and technology are leading the way, enabled by predictive artificial intelligence and innovative companies such as Alibaba.

The Next Disease

While the focus on "disease and cure" solves the short- and medium-term challenges, what happens when a similar zoonotic disease erupts? To meet an increasing demand, wildlife is being sourced from more and more remote patches of the planet. Humans have disturbed these habitats through land use change to satisfy resource consumption needs at the broadest level. More erratic excretion patterns of viruses follow, coupled with mixing of species that increase the risk of so-called "spill over events" that manifest more as a food consumption crisis.

The required solution here is the banning both of wet markets and the eating of exotic animals. This also means challenging masculinities in East Asia and the search for exotic alternative health potions. However, mere legislation will not solve the day. We need to ensure that those trading in these lucrative areas—the bounty hunters—find new work, otherwise, the trade will just go underground. This again is not just a Chinese national issue, but one requiring a global coordinated effort. This in turn will require Interpol to begin to shift towards becoming Earthpol.

Beyond Meat

Perhaps this is more than just a zoonotic crisis. It is not just wildlife that is the problem, but our consumption patterns. Many blame factory farming and warn that the next pandemic will emerge from how we produce food. Hence, we need to redesign cities and what we eat so we do not encroach on wildlife areas. We also urgently need to change our relationship with meat. While challenging meat may be too much for many, the current production models certainly need to shift.

Leadership and Climate Change

We now know that global focus is possible. Global coordination is possible. Solutions unimaginable months ago are now the new normal. This crisis can be seen as a pre-run, a mock trial, preparing us for the real event—the crisis of climate change. Some of the drivers for the zoonotic disease challenge, such as land use change, are also directly related to climate change. What we learn today, and the changes we need to make today, can be crucial for the world we create. Thus, this crisis is essentially about leadership. Can we ensure the shift to a greener planet? This means moving toward solar energies and ending the fossil fuel era.

The End of Capitalism

As we enter a severe recession, or a seven-year malaise, possibly a global depression, the real issue is economic. Creating a world where money keeps on rolling, and not getting stuck in the hands of a few, becomes urgent and imperative. This is a world where glo-cal solutions are focused on equity and prosperity. One where universal basic income (UBI), free education, health, and housing for all are not the sole concern of the left but are acknowledged as essential for global security. We thus need to challenge the world capitalist system with its mantra of "more, more, more for the few." In this scenario, uneven development distorted by deep global inequity cannot continue. Capitalism dies: we help it disappear.

Most likely this will mean three economic spheres. Global cooperatives, globalized industries, and new markets. It will require global governance if not global government. For many, this means surveillance and the loss of individual liberties. For others, this means the end of identity based on whom one hates and other imagined realities. It means accepting that we are human beings first. Innovative technologies could create stunning wealth for all.

The New Renaissance[5]

This then is a much deeper crisis and challenge.

Our view of ourselves as material beings is being challenged. We can either panic or go deep within and mindfully find peace.

Our view of ourselves as defined by the nation-state is being challenged. Viruses do not care about boundaries nor does nuclearization bring safety.

Our view of ourselves as outside of nature, as separate from Gaia,[6] is being challenged.

Our view of ourselves as defined by economics only is being challenged. More and more will recognize and identify with the "**Growth Delusion**."

The deep challenge lies in fixing the great imbalance. In our four spheres of life: economy, society, spirit, and nature, we have overly favored one at the expense of others. We need a great Gaian rebalance, moving to a world with a quadruple bottom line: Prosperity, Purpose, People, and Planet.[7] The current crisis can help us create a new Renaissance—a transformation of self and society, home and planet. There have been two historical renaissances. The Asian classical Renaissance was personal: the quest for inner peace and enlightenment. The European Renaissance challenged dogma, allowing science and art to flourish, creating the possibility of revolution after revolution against authority that does not serve.

We are in a similar process now. However, after the vaccine is found, there will be a push to go back to what we know, the used future. If we are not careful and purposeful, it will be a pause followed by the pursuit of light-speed economic growth—back to where we were. Gaian leadership at this time is about charting a new direction, exploring scenarios, and creating global systems that help us arrive at a new future.

- *What do you see as the critical enablers of your preferred short-term and long-term future?*
- *How will you and your organization chart a new direction, explore possible scenarios, and help to create global systems that enable a new future?*
- *What historically significant event could you draw inspiration from that could create a new post-pandemic Renaissance?*

Sohail Inayatullah is the UNESCO Chair in Futures Studies at USIM, Malaysia; professor at Tamkang University, Taiwan; and a researcher at Metafuture.org, a global think-tank. His recent books include Asia 2038: Ten Disruptions that Change Everything; PROUT in Power: Policy Solutions that Reframe Our Futures; and Transformation 2050. sinayatullah@gmail.com

A Laboratory for the Future

By Liselotte Lyngsø

The pandemic gives us an amazing opportunity to kick-start our experimentation with the world of tomorrow. What areas of life could change for good?

This chapter explores five insights into societal changes that could shape society beyond the war against the virus. Never in recent history have so many people changed their behavior to such a great extent and in such a short space of time as we are witnessing right now. Trends that were already emerging are suddenly being magnified. Families have to adapt to spending time together in a whole new way. Workplaces have to learn to work together—apart. New rules apply. The world has involuntarily been turned into a future laboratory. The pandemic gives us an amazing opportunity to accelerate our experimentation for the world of tomorrow. So, what's on the near horizon?

1. ***Our belief in experts will be reinvented***—We have been through a long period of living with terms like "fake news," "alternative truths," and "post-factual society." A period where integrity did not matter as long as the story was good. However, we are now in the midst of a situation where fact-based specific knowledge is everything. The criteria for having an opinion and contributing is based on professional proficiency

and not the number of likes, followers on Instagram, or the ability to shout the loudest.

Experts are people with a specific and profound insight that we can all benefit from. We already knew this. We just forgot it in the midst of social media's overload of influencers and opinions. The fact that we have now rediscovered some ways of telling the difference between true and false will be crucial for our opportunity to solve other important questions, for example the climate crisis.

2. *From hospitals to health at home*—We've been put in a situation where we're forced to take responsibility for our own health. Am I sick? Do I have a fever? No one dares to cough anymore except—only when they're alone. We stay at home as much and as long as we can, avoiding admission to hospital at any cost. Hospitals are only for very, very sick people! Not us!

    Do-it-yourself health will require that our knowledge about our own wellbeing increases dramatically. We will all have to monitor our temperature, our breathing, and our state of general health. This will raise a number of ethical questions. Will the data that we collect be private or public? Should we let our employer know if our smartwatch predicts that we're coming down with a cold? Should we tell our grandmother that our phone notified us that our Tinder date on Friday night turned out to be contagious?

    Can future employers, the health system, or insurance companies demand that we use technology to monitor our health? Either way, we will likely see an explosion of voluntary self-monitoring and diagnosis so that we—and our surroundings—can handle anxiety, breakdowns, and colds before they occur. Expect new concepts to help us to stay healthy including home hospitals, tele-medicine, 3D printed pharmaceuticals, and personalized health hacks.

3. *We will learn to react to invisible and remote danger*—For a while, the virus was only in Wuhan. Few nations nearby, mostly in Asia, had foreseen that it would spread from China

to the world. The rest of us couldn't see the disease and we couldn't understand it. We couldn't feel the destiny of the Chinese population in our own life and that is exactly the point. Many of the challenges that we will meet in the future won't be visible to us before they knock on our door and, in most cases, that will be too late.

For many years, we have spoken about exponentiality without really understanding what we were talking about, other than a mathematical formula that could lead to disruption. Now, we all get to experience the exponential curve the hard way. This understanding will be an advantage when the technological revolution really kicks in. It will hopefully help us when the ice caps begin to melt with accelerating speed, and we're forced to adapt quickly to rising sea levels and advancing climate change. We've all been given a lesson in why it's so important to act straight away and not to wait for the tipping point.

4. ***By pushing the exit button, we'll practice being the main characters of our own lives***—Netflix, HBO, and all the other streaming services are really making the big bucks these days. Perform your civic duty: stay at home on your couch. Do it for your country. This is a sneak peek into a future where more and more people risk becoming passive bystanders, albeit with a high level of entertainment and constantly improving content. But it's still binging. Infotainment bulimia.

The winners in this vision of tomorrow will be those that manage to keep a focus on whatever helps them to thrive and develop. Are we learning to speak a new language? Are we redecorating? Are we signing up to help out in our community—if we're allowed? We have to enhance our mental strength to not get overwhelmed by the constant breaking news, and instead take control over our lives. The pandemic crisis is our chance to develop our collective ability to focus and participate at a time when the world is extremely alluring, uncertain, and noisy.

5. ***Our curiosity about other cultures will increase***—For years and years, we've talked about the global village. The moon landings and events like the Olympics have made the world seem smaller. Now, we have had the joint experience of being allies at war against a virus. This stands in sharp contrast to our role as victims of a political and ideological trade war between the US and China, with destructive accusations being thrown back and forth.

    We might not be able to travel physically, but the pandemic has made us interested in getting to know each other at a much deeper level. How are other nations and cultures coping with isolation? How are they doing in Spain? What are the solutions in South Korea? Have they stopped kissing each other on the cheek in France? How are the Italians burying their loved ones? Is it really true that the Chinese have been able to contain the infection?

    Perhaps we will, after all, become global citizens who get inspired by other countries' ways of doing things. The great international institutions have, with their silence, left us to draw our own conclusions. Everything has been turned on its head right now. But there's one thing that I'm certain of, our experience of navigating through the pandemic will improve our ability to sense and navigate the future.

- *Are you becoming more critical with regards to the quality of your news flow?*
- *What plans are you making for taking personal responsibility for your own health monitoring?*
- *How is your sense of exponential development, globalization, and interdependence developing?*

Liselotte Lyngsø is managing partner of Future Navigator. Liselotte works extensively with scenarios for the future, innovation, technologies, and megatrends that have consequences for the way we think, work, feel, and behave. She also delivers keynote speeches all over the world. Born in Denmark, she has an M.Phil. in Economics and Politics from St. Antony's College, Oxford University, UK. lll@futurenavigator.com

World War Contagion— Strategies in the Fight Against Our Common Enemy

By Miranda Mantey

What might the world become when the greatest war in recent history isn't with an enemy state, but with a pandemic?

On October 5ᵗʰ, 1937, US President Franklin D. Roosevelt gave a speech while dedicating a bridge amidst rising geopolitical tensions. In a bid to avoid another global war, Roosevelt used this speech, later coined the "Quarantine Speech," to flip around the popular isolationist ideology held by many Americans at the time. He instead urged for the "quarantine" or isolation of aggressor nations. If war were to occur, Roosevelt said, it would threaten the foundation of civilization and lead to a world where there is "no safety by arms, no help from authority, no answer in science."

Fast forward almost 100 years and we are facing another war—not with an enemy that is dividing the world, but a pandemic that is uniting us. Many countries have enacted actions similar to the US Defense Procurement Act to force manufacturers to produce medical equipment. At the same time, economies have virtually been shut down, social distancing has been demanded or encouraged, and curfews or lockdown orders are enforced. We are finding no safety in arms, no answer in science, and are risking losing more lives than in World War One. What will it mean for our future when the biggest war in recent years wasn't fought with an enemy nation, but with a pandemic?

Surveillance has been seen by many as a key mechanism for combating the pandemic—but raises many issues. Previous national surveillance programs such as Black Chamber, Project SHAMROCK, and the Patriot Act were all created in response to wars or acts of terrorism. Black Chamber was born out of World War One and was the first peacetime cryptanalytic organization and the precursor to the National Security Agency (NSA).

Project SHAMROCK was born out of World War Two to monitor all telegraphic data and was part of the Armed Forces Security Agency which later rolled into the NSA. The Patriot Act was born out of 9/11 and outlines the federal government's surveillance liberties in the name of combating terrorism. These programs remained in place beyond the timeline of the perceived threat, not because the event occurred, but because there was a reminder that we had something to fear. In a bid to make sure we weren't equipping our human enemies for success, communications were monitored. Now in many countries, to make sure we aren't equipping our pathogenic enemy for success, our location is being monitored.

Work from Privacy International has found that telecommunication location tracking is being utilized in 24 countries and location tracking for contract tracing or quarantine enforcement is being utilized in 14 countries. The US government is also working with the private sector to analyze aggregate data of people's movements. Will this interest in location data last? It has before. Brown University found that the "US used post-9/11 terrorist fears to expand its monitoring of US citizens who have nothing to do with terrorism." Edward Snowden warns that this event will be an excuse for more surveillance tracking.

The difference between previous surveillance programs and today is that citizens are acutely aware of the government's intent and of their own rights. This concern has been highlighted by Amnesty International's release of recommended conditions to safeguard human rights and prevent surveillance overreach. We are opening ourselves up to a future where our location data can be accessible at any time in the name of safety. However, an uprising against this movement could also occur.

There may be protests, watchdogs, and location data mining scandals, but the biggest challenge will come from the backlash against the potential for corporate misuse of our data through surveillance capitalism. Concerned over the reputational impact, corporations may seek to take positive action to address emerging consumer privacy demands. Over the coming years, many companies may prioritize data privacy, and put ethics at the forefront of software development. This could see them utilize decentralized technologies and leverage innovative governance models such as data trusts to ensure minimal surveillance and prevent data abuse. Nonetheless, the next significant fear-causing event will be a test as to whether this is a marketing facade, or a true cultural shift.

In times of war, not only do we survey, but we also protect. This war against disease is ravaging the lives of people and the lifeblood of economies. Research from the Centre for Economic Policy Research has shown that governments tend to turn to protectionism when facing severe economic downturns. President Trump has restricted the export of medical supplies, shifted domestic manufacturing to help the cause, and has reportedly considered militarizing the longest demilitarized border in the world. Although we all have one common enemy, it can come in the form of innocent foreigners.

Responses to this pandemic threaten to plunge us into a world of isolationism, where countries will truly know who stands by their side in times of crisis. The future will likely see more domestic manufacturing of essential products such as medical supplies. Proximity, guarantee of service, and access to goods will be a priority for cornerstone products rather than the traditional prioritization of low-cost, low-inventory, just-in-time delivery. After the demonstrated lack of support and coordination between allied countries, affluent citizens may well look to prioritize purchasing products from domestic companies in a display of loyalty. North American relations could weaken, with Canada and Mexico diversifying suppliers to involve more Trans-Atlantic trade.

The world will also be looking to honor the heroes of this war—those that have risked their lives for the greater good. Unlike wars in the past, those who have risked their lives are not soldiers but medical personnel and essential workers. Medical professionals are receiving nightly applause, grocery store staff are getting drive-by salutes from first responders, and this respect will likely go on long past the battle. There may be a holiday in their honor, they may receive tax benefits, and they may be recognized at sporting events.

However, the accolades come with challenges. Just as with veterans, post-traumatic stress disorder (PTSD) may be a struggle for those that worked in the hospitals during the pandemic. Many watched not only their friends and family die but also their co-workers. Essential workers are a group which is disproportionately composed of lower-income individuals. Many may feel resentment, as their "decision" to work didn't come from a place of altruism but from a place of financial necessity. Social tensions may also rise as post-pandemic data shows disproportionately high death rates in certain racial groups and lower-income communities. However, one of the greatest outcomes is that we as a society may finally give those that protect our community the same respect as those that defend it.

Guy Ryder, Director-General of the International Labour Organization, said that this pandemic "is the greatest test for international cooperation in more than 75 years." It is very rare that the entire world has one common enemy—an enemy that attacks from within our borders not outside of them. The post-pandemic future will be a test of how fear interplays with surveillance, a test of isolationist and protectionist mentalities, and a test of how we demonstrate gratitude to those on the frontlines. Maybe Roosevelt didn't mean it quite so literally when he said, "war is a contagion," but his words have never echoed truer than they do today.

- *How might companies integrate cyber security and privacy into marketing strategy to develop trust with their consumer base?*

- *Will the pandemic shift domestic purchasing behavior in the longer term and reinforce protectionist policies?*
- *What might frontline workers value most in society's expression of gratitude and support for them in the post-pandemic period?*

Miranda Mantey is an experienced researcher, foresight practitioner, and strategist with a passion for learning and the future. This thirst for knowledge is what led her to her position as strategy and foresight analyst at ATB Financial, where she spends her time monitoring trends to advise projects and innovation strategy. mmantey@atb.com

Five Ways Our Post-Lockdown World Could Change for the Better

By Sheila Moorcroft

What are some of the post-pandemic changes that could bring a fairer future for all?

Since social distancing and lockdown began, life has changed like never before. Economies have shut down, unemployment spiraled, and businesses small and large have failed. Traffic has disappeared, birds are celebrating spring, and people are re-evaluating what is important. As a result, we are doing and seeing things differently, which brings hope of a fairer but more resilient post-lockdown world.

Life Online—From Lifeline to Way of Life

The current crisis has accelerated the growth of life online. Jobs, gym sessions, parties, and food shopping have all migrated online. Cultural institutions, primary care physicians, and schools have all extended their reach into the digital realm.

In a post-lockdown world, remote access will likely continue to be a flexible extension to almost every aspect of life at higher levels than before. This should enable cost reduction, flexibility, new income streams, greater reach, and increased productivity. Employers will be under pressure to facilitate remote working as a regular extension to office-based work. As a result, commuting could reduce, at first because of continued worries about infection, but then to enable greater work-life balance.

Business travel may never return to pre-crisis levels, putting the airline industry and hotels under long-term pressure. Demand for office space could shrink over the coming years as organizations reduce overheads, while retail centers and high streets may have to reinvent themselves even faster to survive.

As a result, digital inequality and universal access to high speed Wi-Fi will be a greater priority, with demand for direct support for the digitally excluded. Big technology companies will be under pressure to be more inclusive, pay a fairer share of tax, and take more responsibility for abuses conducted on and by their platforms.

Rethinking Supply Chains

Nations will need to rethink supply chains to ensure greater resilience. The lack of a domestic diagnostic industry has been cited as one of the reasons why the UK had difficulties in testing and monitoring the progress of the disease effectively. Countries have also been fighting over limited supplies of personal protective equipment (PPE).

Furthermore, global supply chains were seriously disrupted as China's economy shut down. As a result of the pandemic, the era of low-inventory, low-cost supply chains may be over. Companies will need to redesign supply chains for stability and resilience, often bringing supply closer to home. They will need to be more collaborative and less exploitative, working with suppliers in new ways.

Those same shortages have also seen companies large and small repurpose production and innovate to meet demand, going from making perfume and gin to hand sanitizer, and from posh jackets to PPE. Mercedes Formula One and UCL redesigned an existing breathing support machine (CPAP) and achieved production of 10,000 units within a few weeks. This level of innovation, flexibility, and cooperation will be essential to recovery in a post-lockdown world. There needs to be a debate to develop a shared view of national priorities and how to survive not only in a post-lockdown world. For Britain and the EU this debate would extend to surviving in a post-Brexit world.

Valuing Essential Workers

Many jobs—health workers, refuse collectors, bus drivers, care staff, hospital cleaners, delivery staff to name a few—have previously been regarded as low skilled, low paid, and low security. Now they are seen as essential and applauded every Thursday in the UK. The recognition of their centrality to life is already leading to greater demand for, and public support of, better terms and conditions for these workers. The race to the bottom on price for critical services such as social care and cleaning contracts could become a thing of the past. In the UK, that recognition could force the promised rethink of our social care model, so we can genuinely "protect the NHS."

Delivering on these policies means recognizing that quality does not come cheap, that we will all need to be willing to pay. This will mean learning to love tax for what it provides and sharing the burden of meeting the cost of surviving the crisis, while appreciating the benefits this provided to us all. The high levels of unemployment have also forced many to face harsh realities that have previously been remote—something that happened to other people. Now it is a reality for many. Protecting the most vulnerable may include a greater willingness to look at adopting some form of universal basic income (UBI) and increasing security for gig economy workers.

What Did You Do in the Crisis?

Companies' actions during the crisis will be under scrutiny. The extent to which they supported customers or employees or contributed to the common good will be remembered. This may combine with consumers' own re-evaluation of personal priorities—away from high level consumerism and towards experience and survival, shared communication, and appreciation of the small things in life. As we emerge from the crisis, consumers may well reassess brands and companies in the light of their pandemic-time behavior. Expectations of a more inclusive, collaborative, stakeholder-based business model could emerge, where the common good is recognized. The question is how the system will respond to these demands?

Reconfiguring Our Public Spaces

Lockdown has transformed public spaces and places. Streets are safer, cleaner, and quieter. Green spaces are valued as never before. Large crowds in enclosed spaces may be unthinkable for some time. With a vaccine—the only real alternative to social distancing—probably 18 months away, our route out of crisis could be bumpy. We will need to find new ways to stay safe as we try to restart our lives.

Organizations will need to show that they are protecting employees and customers alike. Public spaces across the board will need to be rearranged to maintain distance and reduce the amount of closely shared space. Evidence of deep cleaning and ready access to sanitizer on entering specific places and windows that open will become the norm. More localized ways of living and working, supported by the networks which sprang up during the crisis, could help redesign communities. A move to sustainable, health oriented, walkable urban spaces and building designs may become embedded in new forms of urban planning requirements.

These, and other actions and reactions, could challenge existing economic thinking. They could become a tipping point for wholesale demand for new forms of capitalism and a fairer world.

- *How can your organization include all stakeholders?*
- *What new ways of doing things can you as an individual promote to bring about a more collaborative future?*
- *How can we build resilience and innovation into our organiza-tions and communities?*

Sheila Moorcroft is a director of Realising your Future, where she helps people and organizations make the future work for their business, and their business work for the future. sheila@realisingyourfuture.co.uk

The Pandemic and the Medical Enlightenment—The View from 2035

By Jerry Edling

Looking back from the year 2035, how did the pandemic revolutionize medicine and transform the way the world is connected?

It is difficult to believe that it has been more than 15 years since the pandemic struck. Its impacts sounded straight out of 1970's science fiction, but its effects were deadly. The public policy responses to it were, in some cases, haphazard; but the resolve of people around the world was stalwart. Little did anybody know that the battle against it would trigger a quantum leap forward in healthcare and create a new paradigm for the world economy. From our perspective in 2035, the time of the pandemic seems like the distant past.

Scientists working to end the pandemic turned the normally deliberate protocol of research (papers, peer review, animal trials, and human trials) into a wartime juggernaut. At first, the race to find the cure was competitive: nation against nation, company against company. However, this morphed rapidly into the most active scientific collaboration since the International Geophysical Year (IGY) in 1957 and 1958. The IGY laid the groundwork for the launch of Sputnik 1 and the beginning of the space race. That program took place during a period of higher-than-normal solar activity and led, among other things, to the discovery of the Van Allen radiation belts. The collaboration that began in 2020, led not only to a fuller understanding of the disease, but also to a revolution in our understanding of the genome, genetic mapping, and immunity.

Historically, vaccines have worked by using weakened or deactivated viruses to prompt the body's immune system to recognize them as invaders and act against them. A later technique involved the use of DNA- or RNA[8]-based vaccines that could be produced in the laboratory, digitized, and then transformed into synthetic biological material. That led to a breakthrough that would revolutionize the treatment of pandemics.

The Immunity Revolution

There had long been research into harvesting the plasma of people who had recovered from diseases caused by viruses and were thus immune and then introducing it into other people, so that the antibodies would also render them immune before they were exposed. The technique was effective, the challenge was making it available on a large scale. At the same time, there had been promising experiments in self-spreading vaccines, which are given to some individuals and then spread through populations like pathogens.

The two techniques were then combined to create what one commentator called an "epidemic of antibodies" that could rapidly immunize some populations, especially those in urban areas. The goal was to spread the antibodies before the virus could take hold. Almost universal testing made it possible for public health officials to identify any infections, and apps enabled them to track potential contacts of infected people, who could then be quarantined. So, governments very carefully organized selective social congregation to spread the antibodies. Some theater complexes reopened with invitation-only movie screenings. Public places such as restaurants were open far later into new outbreaks. Needless to say, all of the measures taken to facilitate group immunity were boons to the economy.

However, self-spreading antibodies weren't enough to blanket the planet. Another sort of delivery system had to be used to reach more remote areas. That which led to a revolution in supply chains.

The Innovation Chain

Remember the supply chain? Back in the 2020s it was the nervous system that united the world economy in a web of interdependence. It was fueled by the techno-optimism that prevailed in the first decade of the 21st century, the sense that the Internet would render borders obsolete, dictators helpless, and the world free at last. The exhilaration in those days was breathless. Reality set in, of course, when it was discovered that technology could become as much a tool for oppression as a force for liberation. However, despite the planet's political coming-of-age, the global supply chain thrived, and the world continued to live and spend in fragile interdependence.

When the 2020 pandemic struck, there had been fears initially that a breakdown in supply chains might prevent vaccines from getting to vulnerable populations to end the outbreak. Even then, globalization had its critics, particularly Americans who had lost their jobs when new global trade regimens outsourced the plants that had been their livelihoods. There was a feeling that a new sort of supply chain was needed, one that had global reach but local roots.

That's how the innovation chain came to be. The innovation chain transformed the fundamental business transaction from the purchase of a good to the licensing of a design. This sequential process began with a patent issued in the home country of the inventor. The design of the product was then inputted into the network and exported to local manufacturing hubs in every country, equipped with 3D printers and other additive manufacturing tools. Around 2028, when the devices that could transform digitized genetic code into synthetic biological material were added to these regional manufacturing hubs, antibodies could now be coded and sent anywhere in the world. The manufacturing hubs were nicknamed ATMs for Antibodies, and Rapid Response Immunizations (RRIs) became possible. For the first time in the history of immunization, virtually no one was left behind.

A Medical Enlightenment

Today in 2035, a scientific revolution seems to be taking hold, with the promise of more breakthroughs in the years ahead. Researchers claim they are five to ten years away from the development of a synthetic immune system. This would use artificial intelligence to digitize an individual's immune response to a whole database of diseases and then convert it into a sort of universal vaccine.

The template for scientific cooperation that was established during the 2020 outbreak continues to this day. It has led to a sort of **medical enlightenment** that has consigned some of the most devastating health threats to history. Advances in health and medicine have become a metaphor and blueprint for the development of worldwide solutions to worldwide problems. Science is the search for connections that were previously unknown. Global cooperation is the search for common ground that was previously unexplored.

What a time to be alive.

- *Would the public embrace deliberate and controlled social congregation as a way of spreading immunity before a virus spreads?*
- *Would the innovation chain of globally shared IP and localized manufacturing lead to an age of collaboration and customization?*
- *Could big data be the "magic bullet" that leads to a breakthrough vaccine?*

Jerry Edling is an editor and writer for KNX in Los Angeles and a former editor-in-chief of "Public Diplomacy Magazine." He has been nominated for three Emmy Awards and five Writers Guild of America Awards. He has spoken to the World Future Society and the National Space Society. edlingjerry@gmail.com

Does the Proverbial Cloud Created by the Pandemic of 2020 Have a Silver Lining?

By Paul Plant

What might the long-term societal effects of the pandemic be on today's interconnected world with all its associated pressures on time poverty and lifestyle choices?

There are many quotations about adversity, how good comes from bad, the benefits of perseverance, and how necessity stimulates creativity. As a transformation consultant, I often deliver workshops on business change, and I always kick these off with a session on positive thinking, and how to condition our minds to think differently. Furthermore, the recent surge in uplifting social posts is testimony that people pull together in times of uncertainty, when the "never-say-die" and "in-it-together" mindset takes over; the British sometimes refer to this as "Dunkirk spirit"—a reference to the flotilla of small private boats that sailed from Britain to rescue soldiers from the French beaches during World War Two.

For all the turmoil in the world, there is a widely held view that, for many, when life eventually returns to normal, things will be better than before. In other words, there is hope that we will learn, adapt, and be better prepared. Lessons can be learned from previous major crises, most notably two World Wars, numerous mainly cyclical economic recessions and even the horrific events of 9/11. They all show that many governments, corporations, and ordinary people were better prepared for the future and more resilient after things had stabilized.

To help me understand how people were responding to the 2020 pandemic, I studied a friend's Facebook post, in which they asked people to make three different post-lockdown predictions:

1. What will you appreciate more?
2. What will never be the same?
3. What will be the positive takeaways?

It was hardly a scientific study; however, the post generated a sizable response, with a lot of consistency. I was struck by the amount of thought that went into the answers and what they tell us about how things need to evolve or might change naturally in a post-pandemic world. The Facebook responses touched on political, economic, social, and technological issues, so it makes sense to group them accordingly. In addition to the PEST categories, I have added an extra heading, Individual, as many responses were of a personal nature.

Political

- *Government Transparency*—News travels fast, especially serious, life-threatening news. In today's interconnected world, it's impossible, futile even, trying to hide or cover up bad news. Just as the Soviets tried to keep a lid on Chernobyl, the Chinese tried the same in the early days of this latest catastrophic event. Critical time was lost, yet it is impossible for such diversionary tactics to work. People will generally demand more, clearer, and unfiltered information about important situations.
- *Resilience and Preparedness*—The Boy Scout motto "be prepared" has never been so resonant. Far too many governments, most notably those of the world's richest nations, were ill-prepared for a crisis of this magnitude. It almost defies thinking what might have happened had a terrorist cell or rogue regime initiated a chemical attack, or worse, got access to nuclear

warheads. This latest crisis has brought great clarity to the argument that we need a coherent and coordinated global response network to address such problems.

- *Coordination Infrastructure*—We need better communications infrastructures and support networks. It's not just connectivity or download speed, it's also about the capacity to mobilize resources quickly and efficiently, to the most urgent points of need. Many so-called advanced nations failed in this regard, particularly those with multiple agencies that were not properly integrated or prepared.

- *Key Worker Appreciation*—There is common consensus that greater appreciation, recognition, and reward for key workers is richly deserved. It should no longer be the case that the people we rely on most in times of great need are lowly paid. Nor should it be the case that, far too frequently, they find themselves working in the most appalling conditions with insufficient resources.

Economic

- *Business Growth and Destruction*—The lockdown imperative has unquestionably been a pivotal moment for the ecommerce and home delivery sectors. But it has simultaneously been a wake-up call—or sadly, a death knell—to millions of small businesses all over the globe who thought they could survive without digital communications.

- *Economic Revival*—When the proverbial dust finally settles, it will be critical for governments everywhere to stimulate local economies. Taxation, business rates, employment law, and countless other factors must be reviewed, as communities, towns, cities, and entire nations get back on their feet.

Technological

- *Technology Adoption*—The economic factors, combined with the coping strategies adopted by companies in light of the pandemic, will undoubtedly have implications on future infrastructure, technology adoption and working practices.

The ability of companies to exist with many of their employees working from home will influence changes in organizational structure and operational processes.

- *New Ways of Working*—The sharp rise in video conferencing and technologies that support remote working may possibly lead to a reduction in business air travel. Companies may seek to rebalance their books by cutting unnecessary or non-essential journeys.

Social

- *Community Mobilization*—We have seen a mass outpouring of support for key workers. We've also witnessed communities coming together to help those in greatest need. These acts have proved fairly conclusively that people are generally kind and sympathetic. There is a broad swathe of opinion that a lasting legacy of this crisis will be a heightened respect for frontline workers, which will hopefully be reflected in their remuneration.
- *Enhanced Resilience*—Not only are people generally caring, but also amazingly resilient when faced with an unseen and dangerously lethal threat. There appears to be a collective optimism that we will be better prepared at the individual next time.

Individual

- *Personal Wellbeing*—We have never washed our hands more frequently, been so mindful of personal space, or the impacts of coughs and sneezes. This heightened awareness of personal hygiene has been a timely reminder of the benefits of staying healthy and clean.
- *Use of Time*—The elongated confinement period has encouraged many to undertake a conscious appraisal of how we spend our time. We have shifted from the unproductive—and unhealthy—hours spent commuting, to spending more quality time with children and loved ones. Equally, many are using the extra hours to be more productive, making new discoveries, learning new skills, and getting fit. Some are starting that

book we were always going to write, or just getting back to living life on one's own terms.

We can't yet say what the defining legacy of the latest pandemic will be. Analysts generally believe the world will not simply bounce straight back and that recovery could be a more protracted process. Hence, there is ambiguity around when, how, and what format the recovery will take. However, history dictates that, for many, things could improve beyond pre-pandemic levels.

This small unscientific social study suggests many positives could emerge, not least a greater appreciation for others. We may also see a conscious shift away from the monotonous, energy-sapping routines associated with work and modern lifestyles. Yet above all else, and perhaps the most refreshing prediction, will be a world where we are all more tolerant and kinder to our fellow citizens. Amen to that!

- *What changes to the way you work or conduct your business will stay with you after lockdown ends?*
- *What aspects of your daily routine will be different in future, as a consequence of this enforced period of reflection?*
- *What lasting impressions will your children take away from the global pandemic of 2020?*

Paul Plant is the Chief Listening Officer at Radicle Consulting UK and an experienced strategic marketeer, digital thought leader, and change agent with a track record of transforming and growing businesses all over the world. A former Yell plc executive, he is now an independent consultant, advising on corporate strategy, digital transformation, and customer experience. paulp@winkeepgrow.com

The Case for New Progressive, Socially Focused Economic Initiatives

By Bruce Lloyd

What should be included in a progressive new socially focused, economic and societal recovery agenda?

Countries across the world are facing a challenging time in coming to terms with the implications of the recent pandemic, particularly over the next five years. What is likely to happen? What should happen? For many countries, the priority is very likely to be on returning to the normal patterns of the past. However, I believe what is really needed is to see this as an opportunity to undertake new initiatives that should hopefully lead to a better world for us all in the years ahead.

As has been said many times: "Never waste a good crisis." Although this crisis has been horrendous for many, it is also important to see it as an opportunity for new initiatives—or to provide greater momentum to existing ones. In practice, of course, it is likely that not only should many of the things suggested here happen, but, in many nations, they are quite likely to happen. In addition, it should be recognized that many of the ideas are interrelated and, if combined into a portfolio of initiatives, their impact could be increased significantly. To help initiate discussion, here is a list of ten developments that I believe are required to put us on a more progressive and socially focused path to economic and societal renewal:

1. *A New Strategy*—Develop a coherent package of policies around two key pillars. Firstly, a new global economic recovery plan, similar in philosophy to the US$12 billion "Marshall Plan" enacted by the US in 1948 to help rebuild Western Europe. While the needs for each country would differ in detail, these packages are likely to include some combination of financial support, industry development, skills creation, and debt relief, particularly for nations in the developing world. This support would be provided within governance frameworks established by international financial institutions such as the International Monetary Fund (IMF) and World Bank.

   The second pillar would be new social development program agendas similar to those enacted in 1945 after World War Two by the UK's Labour party to establish a number of universal social provisions that came to be known as the welfare state. These were modeled on ideas proposed in a 1942 report on "Social Insurance and Allied Services" produced by economist and Liberal politician William Henry Beveridge.

   Many such policies are inadvertently having to be pursued by governments of all political persuasion around the world as they seek to prevent the collapse of their economies and civil society. Here in the UK, such policies could well become the priority for the new Labour leader and also for all other parties as they seek to create an economic and social underpinning for recovery.

   Similar pressures are emerging in many other parts of the world, and hopefully this should result in a new global focus for international cooperation, both within Europe and the world as a whole. With a few notable exceptions, the crisis appears to be fostering a new level of global cooperation between experts and professionals. In addition, new technology should help accelerate general societal learning, as well as advancing learning and research to global social and health needs.

2. *Priorities*—Overall, there should be a greater emphasis on the importance of meaning that arises from positive and rewarding relationships, and less on the relatively meaning-less obsession with the accumulation of "things."

3. *Measurement*—A parallel development to point two above is to accelerate the move away from the distorting measure of GDP as an indicator of societal performance. A shift in emphasis is required, with wider use of key social progress indicators, some of which already exist, such as the UN Sustainable Development Goals (SDGs), which should be developed further and used on a consistent basis globally. We should always remember that GDP is essentially an economic measure of quantity, not quality.

4. *Investment*—Much greater emphasis should be placed on driving enhanced wellness and positive health outcomes. This can only be achieved through increased health expenditure on healthcare systems including hospitals, and the care industry. This would involve investment in relevant assets, as well as higher pay for those involved. These should be combined with less expenditure on areas that are more focused on speed, rather than the quality of experiences. Greater emphasis is required on health-related research agendas and less on military indul-gences, such as nuclear missile submarines. Building on the greater spirit of international cooperation should lead to a long overdue new global initiative to eliminate nuclear weapons.

5. *Societal Rebalancing*—The new agenda requires a greater concern for, and investment in, the needs of disadvantaged members of society, both nationally and internationally. Such moves need to be combined with greater pressure for the aboli-tion of tax havens, and higher taxes on the wealth and income

of the richest members of society. It does, however, need to be recognized that many in the rich category will have experienced a disproportionately adverse effect on their income and wealth as a result of this crisis. At the same time, a significant number have also started to acknowledge that their wealth should be used more responsibly.

6. *Environment and Social Responsibility*—A sustainable future requires greater emphasis on investment focused on improving the quality of the environment. This needs to be combined with greater recognition of the need to take issues associated with climate change even more seriously. This would also include business having a greater social agenda within its overall purpose, aligning them more closely with the SDGs. There is also scope for much greater emphasis on the role and importance of social enterprises, including potentially using such models in public service industries such as railways. The goal would be to get the best of management and operational thinking and techniques from both the private and public sectors.

7. *Digital Infrastructure*—Support is required to ensure every citizen can make greater use of the Internet as a means for communication and in the consumption of virtual experiences and services. The pandemic has placed Internet technology at the center of almost every area of our personal and working lives, as evidenced by the rapid shift to online education delivery during the pandemic. This development will increase the pressure for ensuring universal access to technology, investment in driving up digital literacy, and more flexible working in many industries. The expansion of Internet activity will add to the existing trend towards greater globalization of human activity, through video parties, and online learning, that are increasingly location independent.

8. **Leadership**—A more progressive, socially focused agenda implies less emphasis on leadership styles that might be seen as arrogant, opinionated, egotistical, and authoritarian. Indeed, such approaches should not really be considered as "leadership" as a more appropriate word to use for individuals displaying those characteristics would be "boss" or "dictator." In place of such approaches, greater emphasis will be required on a more collaborative approach which recognizes that purpose is more important than the personalities of those involved. Such a move should help improve levels of trust within society —especially when combined with point nine below—as well as the other ideas mentioned here.

9. **Purpose**—There is an urgent need for an overall shift to a world and societies more concerned with values and wisdom as the key measure of personal and societal success, rather than the obsession with money.

10. **The New Normal**—Countries like the UK are establishing groups—sometimes cross party—to focus on the short-term agenda of dealing with the immediate crisis, and how to phase out lockdown in order to get back to "normal." Such groups should also be given an extended brief to cover the development of long-term programs. These should focus on how to achieve a significant shift in our economic and social priorities in a more sustainable direction, to include the areas mentioned above. To expect 100% agreement on the details of such a program would be unrealistic but reaching 80% relatively quickly would be more than sufficient as a basis for action in the immediate future. Identifying the areas of disagreement within the other 20% is also important, and this should then be the basis for future discussion, within and outside the group.

    Although the examples given here come from the UK, the ideas and underlying principles are generally applicable worldwide. There are no perfect answers. However, there are plenty of areas where the development of detailed new initiatives and policies can be integrated into a coherent strategy as a basis for action around these ten ideas. A focus on these can help reassure us that we are not wasting the crisis, and help us all move to a better, fairer, and more sustainable, society and world for future generations.

- *What should be included in progressive, new socially focused economic and social development initiatives?*
- *What are the main barriers to implementing a progressive and socially inclusive global recovery agenda?*
- *How should the implementation process for economic and social recovery be organized?*

Dr Bruce Lloyd is emeritus professor of Strategic Management at London South Bank University. He spent over 20 years in industry and finance before joining the academic world to help establish the Management Centre at what is now London South Bank University. Currently he works part-time for the University, particularly on PhD supervision. brucelloydg@aol.com

SOCIETY AND SOCIAL POLICY

Retroshock—A Return to Roots

By Eleanor "Nell" Watson

How might a post-pandemic return to our roots help take us back towards the stars?

Excerpt from Triumph via Tragedy: A Pandemic Retrospective published June 6th, 2083, Harbin-Tuatini Open Isopress:

74,000 years ago, early humans sheltered in terror, their world torn apart by the aftereffects of the Toba mega-colossal eruption. But those clumsy prototypes of modern man weathered the storm and emerged from it re-forged. They had learned new methods by which to organize their society and to communicate essential knowledge quickly. Thus started critical traditions to underpin a resilient culture.

Our global civilization has never come so terrifyingly close to systemic collapse as in the early 2020s. The plague and its aftershocks of successive crises brought death, despair, and disability to many, along with economic and social chaos that still echo today. But like a forest fire, with the chaff of a smug and sneering society scorched away, the willowy seeds of a wholesome new culture had fertile soil in which to grow.

Crises tend to follow each other like a string of pearls. The lockdowns in China led to massive crop and livestock failures, as food could not be planted, tended, or harvested due to restricted movement of migrant labor, nor could they get to market either. At a time when pigs had already been mass-culled for contracting Swine Fever, and chickens and ducks infected with deadly Bird Flu, animal feed was difficult to source.

During the outbreak, a massive swarm of crop-ravaging locusts descended in successive waves forming a belt all the way from Sudan to Western China, with each wave growing even larger. Greatly diminished air travel led to a lack of jet contrails in the atmosphere, resulting in a climactic whiplash. This saw droughts in dry places and floods in wet ones, followed by inevitable wildfires, dustbowls, and mudslides.

These were unavoidable problems, but the way that humanity initially responded turned them into true crises. A culture of complacency had encouraged people to borrow from the future with a devil-may-care attitude. Social progress had reduced tensions in society, yet paradoxically also increased grievances for trivial affairs. Ideological politicization invaded every aspect of life, with innocent people scapegoated by angry mobs.

Mercifully, the crises changed our course.

So-called experts and pundits were shown to be naked emperors not worth listening to at best and criminally negligent at worst. The institutions relied upon to protect the vulnerable failed when we needed them most. Politics, showmanship, and chicanery swiftly fell out of fashion as people facing harsh realities rapidly became more receptive to basic, timeless, and trustworthy home truths instead.

For the first time in history, all of humanity was truly united against a single foe, in the common interest of our health and bellies, and of keeping the essential elements of society on its rails. Huddled-together-yet-apart, we uncovered the fundamental elements that every one of us shares: good health, treasured relationships, and meaningful activity.

Labor movements and mutual aid organizations formed organically from the bottom-up, bringing a level of crowd-ranked wisdom and level-headedness rarely before displayed in public affairs. These were cultures of gung-ho scrappy hackers finding ways to help remedy awful situations. Running lean, the emphasis of society shifted from seeking efficiency towards flexibility and fairness.

The pandemic shone a spotlight on heroes and villains alike. As people around the world took stock of the elements that enabled the pandemic, they recognized the truest root cause—society was bedeviled by bad actors profiting from shifted costs. Continual cycles of boom and bust were driven by bad actors finding new ways to oblige others to pay for their own costs—from fee riding on publicly funded infrastructure to ignoring the environmental impacts of their businesses. This led to an inevitable collapse of this unsustainable model once people realized the game had been rigged.

Civilization is a tower, each generation adding a new layer of bricks. Sometimes bad bricks get laid, which over time put the tower at risk, especially as the weight above them grows. Every so often, a generation recognizes that a bad brick is so dangerous that its existence can no longer be denied or ignored. It therefore has a duty to carefully demolish a level or two, to replace a bad brick and its surroundings with something better, in order to build more sustainably again.

Globalization had enabled great efficiency, but also terrible fragility, i.e. a cost deferred to the future for a benefit today. The Pied Piper's services had been enjoyed, but not paid for. Cross-partisan movements formed a coalition demanding fair play—urgent reforms in how society accounts for and redresses shifted costs. Never again would society allow fragility, or any other shifted costs, to be created but not offset immediately.

Our global systems have stumbled on two further occasions since 2020, but they have endured thanks to a prepaid network of incentives working to mitigate them.

Civilization is built upon the labors of those who toil for something that they themselves may never realize. Those planting a sturdy tree whose shade they will never know. People began holding each other accountable in saving for a rainy day, and absolutely refusing to borrow from the future.

With plenty of free time at home, people took that planting meme to heart. Victory gardens with fast-growing plants and edible flowers became endemic, with chicken coops an invaluable source of precious protein as well as fertilizer. Ugly vegetables were no less delightful in one's belly and many who harvested them were former office workers. Experiments in baking sourdough bread out of desperation helped people rediscover the great flavors that processed food once denied them.

In this new worldview that respected real food, organic mulch became a valuable commodity rather than mere waste. Difficulties in getting rid of inorganic waste brought people face to face with the inefficiencies of our consumption. Ingenuity shared online invited one to reuse or upcycle instead.

The inability to wander in search of stimulation obliged us to look for it in others. To pick up the art of conversation once again or get lost in a favorite old book. People chose with care and agency with whom, and how, they wished to live their lives. Friends moved in together, as parents discovered the joys of raising children outside of the hustle and bustle of daily life. Adult children appreciated the practical wisdom of their parents, as the older generation smiled in quiet awe at the ingenuity and adaptability of their offspring.

Eventually, as the dust began to settle, a new normal emerged, a world not quite as complex and fancy as the old one. But very few wanted to return to how things were before, even if they could. Something had changed in each of us—we had discovered our roots, the things that give life meaning. The refocus was towards honest work, mutual reliance in trusted networks, and a return to the fundamentals of common sense and human decency. People rediscovered the simple country wisdom of minding one's own business but being there for a neighbor when needed.

As the decades drew on, humanity crept forward once again towards automation and global integration, but this time in a sustainable, slow, and savoring manner. Chastened as we were after the horrors of World War One and World War Two, we resolved that the third time would be the charm. Eradication Day, that closed the World War Three chapter of humanity versus virus, marked the dawn of a new world.

Never again would we permit bare-faced deceptions, sneering contempt, and feckless irresponsibility on such a scale as in the first two decades of the 21st century. The reforms and wisdom born from our difficult struggles have stuck around. They enable us to live sustainably without robbing each other.

Finding our roots made all the difference. Having put our house in order, it's time for us to reach again for the stars.

- *If you designed your life with only happiness in mind, what might it look like?*
- *What would happen if all of the true costs to society of a product, service, or business process were included in its price?*
- *What new institutions could prevent a pandemic tragedy from occurring again?*

Eleanor "Nell" Watson CITP FBCS FICS FIAP FIKE FRSA FRSS FCMI FLS is a tech ethicist, machine learning researcher, and social reformer with a longstanding interest in making sense of the nuances of complex systems, and how we might better align societal incentives. nell@nellwatson.com

Policing the New Normal

By Katherine Van Gurp and Mike Richmond

What forces could shape the new normal of policing in the post-pandemic world?

The current global pandemic is one of the most significant challenges humanity has faced, with significant loss of life and cascading impacts through global and domestic socio-economic systems. In reality, we are actually dealing with two crises—the health threat itself, and the economic crisis caused by the restrictions put in place to combat the pandemic.

Globally, police have been catapulted into unfamiliar public health roles. In Australia and New Zealand, as elsewhere, police have mobilized rapidly to meet this challenge and manage the risks to their workforces' wellbeing, at the same time as cascading impacts have altered the criminal landscape.

What is increasingly clear is that while police energies are focused on managing the present, the new normal that emerges from the pandemic is likely to be substantially different to the normal we left behind.

People Power

Policing is about people, and undoubtedly the pandemic has the potential to shift the dynamics between individuals and groups, and the flow of people within and between countries for years to come. Successful strategies to manage the outbreak have been contingent on the ability for (national) communities to act with a collective spirit to achieve public health outcomes. In response, many governments around the world have adopted war metaphors to mobilize public attitudes.[9]

This collective spirit might endure with positive benefits to social norms that can help prevent crime.[10] There have, however, been reports that many social[11] and ethnic[12] divisions have deepened in recent months, due to uneven experiences of infection or employment outcomes. Further, some accelerationist groups have reportedly sought to deliberately spread the virus amongst vilified minorities.[13]

Urban landscapes could also shift, with increasing preference for private modes of transport[14], impacting road safety—particularly in jurisdictions with high proportions of public transport use. Enduring anxiety about the risk of infection on crowded public transport routes could also see spikes in violence and public order issues.

International and inter-regional transportation is also likely to be affected for many years. It is highly likely there will be strict health checks on crew and passengers, and it is possible "proof of immunity" could be required at borders. Such impacts are also likely to affect migration, which is particularly problematic for countries like Australia and New Zealand where migration and tourism contribute significantly to economic growth.[15]

Money Matters

The economic crisis is likely to have significant and enduring impacts. Many governments are currently deploying unprecedented levels of stimulus to keep their economies afloat, but many people are also experiencing life-changing economic stress. Women, younger people, and low-income households so far seem to be disproportionately affected by job losses.[16]

On the surface, sustained financial stress can increase the risk of property crimes, but at a deeper level, the post-pandemic world could see a variety of impacts of rising economic inequality. Young people might perceive an inequity in bearing the brunt of economic impacts for older and wealthier generations and the prospect of lower living standards, which may erode trust in institutions, manifesting in public protests. [17,18]

Police budgets could also be impacted in future. While law enforcement may be prioritized over other services, given the range of factors that shape crime, reduced funding to other services could result in criminal activity down the track.

Digital Diaspora

Social distancing measures have forced many of us online to work, study, and socialize. The longer the crisis endures, the more the Internet will be entrenched as the primary social medium. However, such a shift comes with risks. Heinous crimes like child exploitation have already flourished in online spaces, and it is likely such offenses will increase with the expanding use of the Internet. Such a future also increases cybersecurity risks. Already there are reports emerging of increasing phishing, frauds, and other cyberattacks on vulnerable systems such as the health sector for ransom or to exfiltrate personal data.[19]

This shift will pose many challenges for policing, particularly as such crimes often straddle international borders, making them difficult to investigate. It will see the scale of those challenges increase, and new strategies will be needed—including deeper partnerships with social media platforms, banks, and other private sector organizations with large data holdings.

Trust Talks

The ongoing shift to the digital-first world has added fuel to concerns about increasing authoritarianism based on the extraordinary powers many governments have granted themselves, and their police, to combat the pandemic.[20,21]

Work is underway to develop contact tracing methods that do not impact privacy.[22] While relationships with authority vary across individuals, communities, and nations, we know that trust is critical to both governments and policing. Low trust increases the cost of doing business.

Some governments will wind back powers as the virus subsides and some will not. Regardless, it seems highly likely that trust will become even more important for the social contract between the public and authorities in future than it was pre-pandemic.

- *What pressure points are shaping future safety outcomes in your hometown, city, or country?*
- *What new vulnerabilities might emerge amongst the people in your hometown, city, or country?*
- *How can you support positive public safety outcomes for your community in the years ahead?*

Katherine Van Gurp is the Chief Executive Officer of the Australia New Zealand Policing Advisory Agency (ANZPAA). Katherine has over 25 years' experience working across a range of law enforcement and justice agencies in Australia at the Commonwealth, State and Territory level.

Mike Richmond leads the strategic foresight program at ANZPAA, providing regular environment scans and trends analyses to police leaders that foster strategic discussion about current and emerging challenges. mike.richmond@anzpaa.org.au

This IS a Drill—Preparing for the Next Pandemic

By Morgan D. Kauffman

What if the world carved out a time for a quarantine drill every other year, both to cut the transmission of normal diseases and to prepare for the next pandemic when it inevitably strikes?

There are hundreds of infectious diseases that circulate endlessly within the human population, ranging from the common cold to serious diseases like measles. Some of these, like malaria, also have animal hosts, but many exist mostly or only in humans. If we could periodically put a halt to their transmission from one person to the next, we could greatly reduce the human cost and the economic impact of these endemic diseases.

That might seem impractical. After all, we've lived with these diseases for a long time. But what if we could break the chain of transmission for these diseases, while also setting up and practicing a national and global response for serious epidemics and pandemics?

"Yes ma'am, it looks like there's a package sold by the grocer near you that's covered by the subsidy," I said into the headset microphone.

"Yes ma'am, gluten-free, low-sodium. They've got 4.8 stars on the rating site. How many people will be quarantined with you?"

"All right, I've got you down for four weeks' supply for three people. You'll be getting the receipt in your inbox shortly and the pallets should be delivered by Wednesday. Was there anything else I can help with? You've got all your prescriptions squared away?"

"Okay, wonderful, you stay safe, ma'am. Bye!"

I pressed the button to hang up and sat back with a sigh. Working phone duty in late January on a Q-Month year got hectic, what with everyone panicking and realizing that they didn't actually have enough food to last the next month without a trip to the store. Or, God forbid, someone didn't have enough toilet paper stocked up; the Internet could get positively vicious in its mockery whenever a story like that got out.

After four successive drill cycles, people were finally starting to get used to what was involved in prepping for Q-Month. Store enough food, supplies, medications, and entertainment to spend all of February without venturing outside your house or apartment, aside from a solitary walk or run. If your job doesn't let you work from home, try to find a hobby that will keep you entertained without driving your housemates crazy. Make damn sure that your Internet and phone service are set up properly so that you don't go the last two weeks without.

Still, some folks will always have trouble with parts of it, and that's what my job was for—straightening out the wrinkles so that we could have an effective quarantine drill. It defeats the purpose if people still ventured out in search of a forgotten inhaler refill, or if they ran short of food in the last week and had to go and buy more. After the first Q-Month's utter train wreck, the government set up the call centers and gave us the task of fixing people's problems.

During most of the two-year interval between Q-Months, our role was more about logistics than anything. Our job was ensuring that the supply lines for the Q-Parcels were functioning smoothly, flagging any issues with product quality, and making sure that the national stockpiles of medical supplies were ready to go if a pandemic hit unexpectedly. But then December and January arrive and, despite doubling up on people, we still can't answer the phones fast enough.

Got a landlord threatening eviction or refusing to fix the plumbing just before shutdown? Call us to flag him for an investigation. Don't have enough food and you're not sure which distributor of prepackaged quarantine supplies qualifies for the government subsidy? Call us and we can set you up. Although honestly, you could do just as well on the national Q-Month logistics website. The Q-Shift substitute for your grandmother's home healthcare aide is sick and had to cancel? Okay, that's harder, but we can still connect you to a non-profit in your area that will help you find a replacement.

Things really go into high gear in January with the general population calling in, but the calls start coming in early December when the Q-Shift teams start stocking up. Those are the folks who have volunteered to work at essential posts like hospitals, utilities, and distribution centers during February when the rest of the world is shut down. But to do that, they need to self-isolate for the last four weeks of January so that they can be sure they aren't bringing anything infectious to work. That means they need to start preparing in December.

All the logistics headaches have been worth it though. When the Chicken Flu broke out in '25, we had stockpiles in place to deal with it, and people already knew what to do. Sure, the economy took another hit, but it was just a minor stumble rather than the crash that happened in 2020. More importantly, people were only in their homes for one month, rather than the multiple months it took to get widespread testing set up after the mishandling of the 2020 outbreak.

The corporate lobby howled like demons during the act's passage, but nowadays there's not so much of a peep of protest coming out of them. National productivity was up substantially last year, mostly thanks to fewer people calling in sick. The best estimates are that just cutting the spread of the flu has added 0.4% to GDP growth and saved 30,000 lives per year, and cutting colds from an average of four per year down to one added another 0.2%. Not to mention how it's cut down on the spread of normal influenza and colds.

All of those numbers should continue to improve as more countries join us. We already have most of Europe, East Asia, and the Western Pacific, plus Canada, Mexico, Chile, and Peru. Mandatory health checks and other restrictions on travel from non-compliant countries are putting increasing pressure on them to join in. The closer we get to a truly global Q-Month, the closer we get to eliminating some of these endemic diseases, or at least reducing them to minor nuisances. And the better prepared we all will be for the next pandemic!

- *How might society respond to periods of quarantine being implemented as a means to manage or even prevent future pandemics?*
- *What would be necessary to make mandatory bi-yearly pandemic quarantine drills possible, without crippling the economy or harming vulnerable populations in a country or worldwide?*
- *What might the mid-point be between mandatory pandemic bi-yearly quarantine drills and no public preparedness?*

Morgan D. Kauffman is a futurist, systems modeler, and data scientist with experience in consulting and writing about climate, inequality, tax and welfare systems, and public policy.
morgandkauffman@gmail.com

Preparing for a New Way of Being

By Julia Paulette Hollenbery

Can we relax when we don't know what is going on?

Unknown

Right now, the only thing that is certain is that everything is uncertain. We know relatively little, any of us, as to how this pandemic and lockdown response will play out in the next months, years, and decades across the world and for our neighborhoods and families. In short, we are in a dramatic new normal, a contemporary chaos, an unfamiliar unknowable landscape.

Mind Boggling

We are trying our best to make sense of what is happening to us now, but these are just attempts at meaning-making, at order creation. We are busy projecting a hypothesis, for a Newtonian physical cause and effect, or a sensible beginning, middle, and end of the story.

In this unfamiliar and uncomfortable situation, we want to be able to generate certainty, so that we can again feel comfortable and confident. We want to make use of our old way of operating in the world—top down, knowledge library, dominance of others, strategy, and best guess conclusions—a way of functioning that belonged to the old pre-pandemic universe.

Coping with Chaos

However, it seems highly likely that, in the next several months and years, we will see more, not less, chaos. The expectation is that lockdown will bring economic recession or depression, unemployment, and inflation. Many people could lose their income and their primary relationships. A mental health disaster is brewing.

Some people's personal identities and survival strategies will crumble. Who will they be without their money, material possessions, family, and status? When their high-maintenance survival strategies aren't available. When their assumptions are no longer relevant. When the driver is soul not ego.

Psychologically and spiritually, we see that we sometimes have to move through personal breakdown in order to break through into a new way of being that is more real and satisfying. It can be a very challenging process that is ultimately rewarding. Through suffering, we can travel deeper. We can access more wisdom and pleasure.

I believe humanity is moving through something similar now and can, with the right attitude and resources, emerge into a more realistic and more satisfying future for us all.

In Relationship

The pandemic is showing us that despite our ideas of individuality and competition, we all need each other in order to survive. Our health depends on those who collect our rubbish bins, who stack food onto shop shelves, and who can nurse us when we are really ill.

Can we see now that our lives are dependent on the interrelatedness of everyone and everything? Will we realize that the health of the earth depends on our loving care of it? And that without the earth being healthy we, as a part of it, cannot be healthy either?

Changing Our Ways

The old disposable way of life, with fast lattes, cars, food, and sex had us humans center stage, in the most important starring role. In future, will we shift to seeing ourselves as part of a wider interconnected world of health, relationships, and purpose? Will we be able to acknowledge where we have previously gone wrong in our unkind behavior to other people, animals, insects, plants, and the earth itself?

Will we be open to listening to those we have previously dismissed? Will we be willing to respect women and indigenous people, healers, and spiritual teachers? On the edge of mainstream society, these people have lived through difficult times. They learned how to be vulnerable, to shed false ego skins, and emerge soul naked "out-and-proud" into the light. They learned how to live together with the earth. They are the ones who have already walked this path of change; their experience can now guide the majority, if they are willing.

Sensing the Body

In order to navigate this future terrain well, we will need a new human operating system. Our old software, noted, saved, and mapped out what happened to us, in a program that could then reliably predict what would happen to us next. Our minds would reliably predict how other people might behave in a specific set of circumstances. A + B = C

In an uncertain future world, many of the old navigation points we thought were constant, will have changed or be changing. Perhaps there will be other pandemics, or other unexpected system changes, such as the breakdown of our food and water supply, electricity, or the Internet. Old beliefs, habits, and behaviors will not work in a new landscape. We need now to be able to access a different kind of intelligence, which is effective in an unfamiliar setting. We need to be alive and responsive to this moment, with this person, in this unknown situation.

I strongly believe that those who will survive in the future will not be those with the most money or material goods. It will be those who can make use of their own instinctual intelligence, guided by the promptings of their own sensitive body. Those who can speak from, and take action on, arising sensations, impulses, intuitions, and images in connection with input from the natural and human world, heeding the information provided by the context around us.

Creating Our Future

If we can combine the unfolding wisdom of the flesh and the earth, we will be able to relax into trusting the unknown and the wealth of invisible information available to every one of us, all the time. This is a way of walking in the world that is not controlled and defined by us and our ideas. It is about being open, permeable to the biggest intelligence, within which we all are living.

The future is not certain. Not only because we don't know what will happen, but because we ourselves are an essential part of the creation of it. How we respond now, and in the next few minutes, weeks, months, and years will determine it. If we continue to operate only from our anxious programmed minds, we may see more destruction and deaths happening, not less. If we can open ourselves to include rather than exclude, to combine rather than analyze, we may well see a different outcome.

Can we blend body with mind, heart with knowledge, feminine with masculine, destitute with wealthy, insects, animals, plants, land, water, and air with humans and human creations? If yes, I believe we can fashion a fabulously fertile future.

- *Is it interesting or helpful to notice how your body is feeling?*
- *Do you trust your intuition?*
- *How can you care for nature?*

Julia Paulette Hollenbery is a spiritual therapist, embodiment teacher, and author with 25 years' experience working with individuals and groups. She is an expert in living well with fear; having navigated life begun in birth trauma, she now shares beneficial ideas and practices from her healing journey and innate knowing.
julia.hollenbery@gmail.com

Zoomers Learning About Their Roots in History Class

By Sylvia Gallusser

How can we help the generation of Zoomers, resulting from the pandemic "Baby Zoom," to reflect on their roots and define their identity in this new world and paradigm?

History Class, MLK High School, January 2037

"Let's all turn our H-Story pads to page 183, where we left off last time."

Sounds of virtual pages turning filled the classroom.

"As you might recall, to combat the spread of the virus, shelter-in-place was imposed in multiple states across the US, starting in March 2020 with California and New York. Unfortunately, while the measures did curb contamination and death rates, they remained insufficient to prevent the continued spread. The primary sources of contamination were grocery shopping and healthcare facilities. Consequently, new regulations were put into place restricting days and times people could go shopping. Can anyone explain how they were established?"

"First, the elderly could enjoy dedicated timeslots—typically early morning," ventured Rick from the first row. "Then last name became the main criterion, so families could go together."

"Exactly! This new restriction, although not strictly enforced, helped significantly. Numbers started to plateau, and people got hopeful again. But then two critical events took place.

"The first was the premature attempt to relaunch the economy, which had come to a halt almost overnight. Non-essential businesses had to close, and the unemployment rate skyrocketed due to a combination of firings and hiring freezes. To avoid further deterioration of the situation, workers were incentivized to return to work. However, minimal safety equipment was distributed in the workplace—just masks, gloves, and sanitizer. Shelter-in-place was eventually lifted in multiple states, and schools reopened before the situation was completely resolved.

"Secondly, even before the first vaccine was manufactured, a derived strain of the virus emerged. Pharmaceutical efforts were redirected towards the development of a broad-spectrum multi-respiratory syndrome vaccine destined to also protect populations from subsequent virus variations. This, combined with the rushed reopening of the economy, had dreadful consequences, with infection rates and the death toll reaching new highs."

Andrea paused to catch reactions from the students. Despite being part of the boom in births following the onset of the Great Pandemic, they appeared oblivious to the dramatic events surrounding their conception.

"In this crisis, humans were reminded that they remain social animals. People became desperate to leave their home desk, screens, and video-conferencing apps, to hang out with peers, rediscover green spaces, and visit cultural sites again. In Paris, curfew hours for outdoor physical activity were established from 10:00 am to 7:00 pm; on the very first day of implementation, half of Paris rushed to the Quais de Seine for a jog at 7:00 pm, partially defeating social distancing measures. In nursing homes, seniors were cut off, and visits from their loved ones were prohibited."

The facts didn't seem to resonate with her audience—the so-called "Generation Zoom" or Zoomers. Her inability to better convey the profound wounds of that epoch left Andrea frustrated. Even 15 years after the events, mentioning the Great Pandemic still threw shivers down her spine as she recalled the tenseness of her teenage years. She recalled the ever-increasing stress at home after her mom's firing—which HR had called a furlough, as if terminology would sweeten the blow—and then her father's first symptoms.

"In 2021, the stock market continued its plunge. Over 20 million Americans were jobless. Many employees struggled to find a sustainable balance between working from home and home schooling. Domestic violence and divorces peaked. Millions of homes were lost despite government initiatives to safeguard the most fragile populations. The situation was similar in other countries, reaching half a million deaths worldwide and…"

"Was the vaccine still unavailable?"

"Great question, Daryl. Unfortunately, it was. It was a confusing time for medical research. Significant progress was accomplished in the US through private companies and initiatives such as the Bill & Melinda Gates Foundation, but also worldwide, in China, UK, and Germany. However, vaccines take a long time to be developed, tested, and mass produced for eight billion plus people."

Andrea sat down, annoyed with herself to still be so activated as she mentioned the medical aspects of the crisis.

"Let's focus on the sociopolitical consequences. An extensive debate arose as to how to proceed in the face of this invisible adversary. The elections delayed by six months made a messy situation even messier. Politics was really getting in the way of addressing the biggest threat the US and the world had ever faced.

"Mid-2021, the Infectious Disease Task Force launched the Co-separation order, with 'co' standing for the virus' name and not the Latin prefix for 'jointly'. We are all familiar with the still implemented 'Safe-and-separate' rule. But we need to put into context the paradigm shift that occurred when officials decided to break our social spaces in two, and restrict access solely based on health status.

"People were forced into mass testing. Colored badges were issued, green for those who had been vaccinated or recovered, blue for those who had been infected—declared or asymptomatic—but were still potentially contagious. You'd go to different schools, different stores, different bars, and different churches! Some corporations made good PR, advertising diversity policy as they integrated the risky 'blue' subjects—meaning they were parked in the least attractive buildings, ate at separate lunch times, and used different bathrooms."

"Was everything fixed after that?" risked a fidgety student, eager for a recess.

"Yes and no. The main objective of healing the economy was reached. Most businesses were able to reopen. Unemployment finally returned to pre-pandemic levels. Contagion was controlled, given people could only mingle with peers displaying the same health status.

"But the public reacted strongly against the motion, echoing bad memories of the segregation era. Protesters feared that different social classes would receive unequal access to healthcare options and treatments, and that co-separation would lead to a new kind of 'social leper'. This would not be the first time in history that a plague would induce stigmatization and social isolation. The riots grew fiercer, and the government had to enforce the new regulations militarily late in 2021."

Andrea closed her eyes for a second, remembering her freshman year at Berkeley.

"Nonetheless, the motions were ultimately efficient, and this family of virus became as easily treatable as a bad flu. 'Safe-and-separate' has kept us safe up until this date."

- *How might history regard the initial attempts made by major governments around the world to contain the pandemic?*
- *What draconian measures may be required if existing measures fail to prevent a significant second wave of infections?*
- *What existing social structures could be radically changed to manage future contagion?*

Sylvia Gallusser is an inquirer of our future, conducting prospective (foresight) studies on the future of health and aging, and the future of work and learning. She has also explored transformations in transportation and mobility and in the retail world. Sylvia also monitors the future of the mind and transhumanism. sylvia.gallusser@gmail.com

When the Future was Bright

By Joe Tankersley

Are we considering the fullest possible range of unexpected second and third impacts from the pandemic in our rush to return to life as normal?

I've been staring at the back of this woman's head for hours now. As the blistering midday sun beats down on us, I've taken to counting individual strands of graying hair. Every few minutes, we shuffle forward a few feet as they let the next group enter the medical tent that is our destination. Sweat soaks my clothes, all the way down to my socks, causing a squishing noise whenever we move.

The line surges forward again. The woman, taken by surprise, stumbles and falls. A forgotten instinct takes over. I bend down to check on her, touching her gently on the shoulder. She jerks away violently.

"Get off me," she croaks through parched lips.

I pull back. Startled. Guess I shouldn't be surprised that the years of social conditioning are so strong that they work even here. I consider trying to convince her that I pose no threat.

"Keep it moving." A voice from the shape dressed in the orange hazmat suit, rifle slung over its shoulder, cuts short my contemplation. I step cautiously around her and move on. The sound of a boot thudding against flesh is followed by a weak cry. The people in the line behind me have no generosity to spare for the heap on the ground.

Twenty steps forward and we stop again. This is not the future we were promised. Back in the early days of the pandemics, after the reality had set in, we were flooded with promises of better tomorrows. The pandemic would bring out the best in society. The pause would cause us to reconsider our relationship to one another and the planet. This was going to be the great pivot for humanity. All we had to do was work together, be patient, and follow a few simple rules.

For a brief moment, we did follow the rules. We put the giant machine of capitalism on pause. Life slowed down. We even took time to notice the bright blue skies, free of smog. We marveled at the rivers suddenly teeming with fish, or at least the photoshopped images of them online.

But it didn't last. We quickly became desperate to get back to work. Excuses were made, stores reopened; suddenly, every business was essential. Was it greed? Or simply fear of embracing a future that was so radically different? Probably some of both, mixed in with real need and profound denial.

But hey, the economy rebounded. Bigly. Not because the virus disappeared. It turns out the GDP doesn't give a damn if you're making cars or coffins, taking a flight to Disneyland, or going to your grandfather's funeral. It's just numbers and the numbers stacked up. Along with the bodies. But those we just hid inside silent hospital corridors.

So we learned to make the new normal work. To convince ourselves that life was good again. Well, unless you were old or sick, or needed medical care of any sort. The second and third waves of the virus devastated the healthcare system. Many of the medical personnel who escaped the disease were too burned out to go on. So now we stand here in the blazing summer sun. Waiting our turn.

The line moves forward again. I've finally made it to the entrance. Guards in hazmat suits stand aside as exactly 24 of us enter. Once the room is full, the guards seal the entrance. An eerie silence and diffused light coming through the vinyl sides of the tent envelop us. It feels as if we have stepped into a dream world.

Then the sound of hissing as the gas starts to pour from overhead pipes. I smell strawberry. Sickly sweet strawberry that triggers a long-lost memory. Sixteen again, summer days on the banks of a river, drinking cheap wine with my first real girlfriend. The wine and her lips both tasted of sugary sweet strawberries. Such a long time ago. When the future was bright and filled with promise. I smile and breathe deeply to make sure the gas fills my weak lungs. My last hope is that someday my grandchildren and their children will again have the chance to remember a time when the future was bright and filled with promise.

- *Long-term stress on healthcare systems is just one example of a secondary impact from the pandemic. What other external stresses might arise from the pandemic that could impact your business or organization?*
- *Dealing with the pandemic has already required an increase in governmental emergency powers and surveillance. What might be the long-term impact of those decisions on your business or organization?*
- *It is impossible to predict the exact timing and impact of large-scale disruptions, like this pandemic, but that doesn't mean we can't be better prepared for them when they happen. What other natural, social, economic, or political disruptions should we be preparing for now?*

Joe Tankersley is a futurist, author, and former leader of Walt Disney Imagineering's foresight group. He uses the power of narrative to help communities envision futures that are sustainable, abundant, and just. He is a former member of the board of directors of the Association of Professional Futurists and is the author of *Reimagining Our Tomorrows*. joe@uniquevisions.net

Post-Pandemic Homes

By Alexandra Whittington

Will our future home be a protective haven of safety and wellbeing?

This chapter speculates on how our homes could be reshaped by the pandemic experience. The home was a vital place in the 2020 pandemic response. Citizens around the world were asked to stay home under the public health strategy of social distancing and associated governmental lockdown policies. Communities developed various definitions as to what "staying home" entailed. However, around the world it meant one thing that we all shared in common: a lot of time spent in one's place of residence. Unless an effective vaccine or treatment is developed in the foreseeable future, this could be true for 18 months or more.

Even more concerning is the fact that diseases of all kinds are expected to worsen as a result of climate change.[23] Although the pandemic has afforded the planet a respite from business as usual with much manufacturing and mass transportation on hold, we still face ecological fragility. Furthermore, regular ecological crises over the past several years mean that many parts of the world have already grown accustomed to repeated "shelter-in-place" events in response to the resulting extreme natural disasters. The pandemic is perhaps just another worrying thread in a web of interconnected problems that place us at risk and seeking refuge at home.

Although the pandemic of 2020 will eventually end, the question arises of how might the home evolve as a result of the lockdown experience? Specifically, the pandemic has raised our awareness of the ability of a microorganism to bring modern life to a standstill. This fact alone could impact home design choices and lifestyle planning. Has the pandemic, along with other dangers such as climate change, promoted a trend of cozy home "cocooning"[24] into a form of survival?

Safe Spaces

During the lockdown period, people made the most of whatever resources they had to interact with each other and the wider outside world—ranging from teleconferencing equipment and social media to handwritten signs in windows and singing from our balconies. In particular, many had to carry on working and schooling from home, often in less than ideal circumstances. Is it possible that, in the next few years, residents could convert spare space into media rooms for use during lockdowns? As a step up from the standard home office, a media room would contain a green screen, soundproofing, good lighting, and computer equipment ready for use in classes, meetings, and webinars. In addition to work and education, proper exercise facilities also may become very desirable where inhabitants expect to spend a lot of time at home.

Employers, school systems, and community funds might make grants and loans available for adequately equipping and upgrading the technology in our homes for future lockdowns. Equally, employers might fund such expenses for their staff and governments might provide tax relief on the cost of purchase or rental of services such as broadband and 5G.

A preference for telecommuting, that was developed during the pandemic, could result in many employees deciding they are never going back to the office. The office may not be there for some people to go back to, either, as companies decide to cut their risk exposure: a remote workforce does not transmit illness and reduces the amount of office space required. A home with an extra room is a luxury that may evolve into a status symbol should it soon become a necessity for coping with conditions where most people choose, or are compelled, to stay at home. Clearly, there is a risk of heightening social inequality for those who cannot afford such solutions.

Clean and Sanitized

Whether or not there is a pandemic going on, we want our homes to be safe and clean. There are a number of technologically advanced air purifiers, robotic vacuums, and various smart appliances already on the market to help maintain a tidy modern home. In the future, as pandemics perhaps perpetuate or intensify, it may be desirable to not just clean but actually decontaminate spaces, ourselves, and our belongings that have been outside of the home. For example, shoes and outerwear that came in contact with the street could be routinely sanitized with light or heat emitted by the entry room walls or doorway.

The advent of Internet of Things connection makes it entirely possible that home hygiene devices could also connect both to sensors in our clothing and to tracking and tracing programs implemented at community, city, and regional levels. A smart home assistant could instantaneously notify the residents of viral contaminants on a jacket, new infections nearby in the neighborhood, or provide in-home antibody testing. Such developments might make some people feel safer—and everyone else feel like they are living with Big Brother.

Beyond gadgets, there could be growing consumer demand for furnishings and fabrics to decontaminate the home. Textiles with natural or synthetic disinfectant properties could gain popularity. Could a front door entry mat clean the bottom of your shoe when you walk in the house, for example? As society becomes intimately familiar with the lifespan of various microorganisms, the surfaces which neutralize viral and/or bacterial threats may be favored in the home. For example, wood is naturally antibacterial while traditional carpet is known for capturing dust and mildew. Another key consideration for home shopping decisions would be how to keep chronic illnesses at bay. Enhancing the immune system through unusual design techniques like color, lighting, or feng shui could be embraced.

Contact-Free Consumption

During the pandemic period, consumers had to figure out how to get the things they needed during lockdown, often without leaving home. Online shopping, subscription shopping, ecommerce, and drive-through/takeaway/curbside services have flourished as a result. The desire to have "contact free" delivery may evolve to the point where people adapt outdoor spaces on front steps or porches with secure and antibacterial containers to receive deliveries. Autonomous delivery vehicles from robots and drones to driverless vehicles could play a role in keeping risks even lower. There could also be a break-through in germ-free packaging materials, possibly made from organic compostable materials to offer the ecological touch. Other consumers might go high tech with personal UV light wands to detect and zap contaminants on their mail or parcels.

Whatever the strategy, it is very possible that people are going to be more aware of the fact that there is a supply chain at work and that items have been touched by many hands before they reach the home. Furthermore, consumers are gaining a perspective on the risk that delivery workers take in the course of their jobs. Planning ahead for purchases and showing respect for the logistics of obtaining what is needed, may become an important aspect of consumer behavior in the next few years, particularly while lives are on the line. The pandemic might accelerate the rise of employee-free stores like the cashier-less Amazon Go store, making it safer for essential employees while they work to ensure people get what they need at home.

Conclusion

The pandemic created an unexpected lockdown situation that resulted in novel changes to the home environment, mostly designed to prevent the spread of a seriously contagious virus. How much of it will stick around into the near future? Is the pandemic putting the "cocooning" trend on an exponential path that will eventually transform the home from a cozy haven into an impermeable fortress? Will we continue our vigilance against microscopic invaders, or can we expect the antibacterial craze to end as the risks dissipate? Can we carry on with school and work under lockdown and shelter-in-place orders—and do some of us prefer it that way? The outcome will surprise us, but the resiliency of the human species will not.

- *Could in-home smart devices help with the process of tracking and tracing infected individuals?*
- *Should the home of the future be self-sufficient?*
- *Which adaptations made to our lives during the pandemic should be carried forward into the future?*

GOVERNMENT AND ECONOMY

Post-Pandemic Government—A Futurist Perspective

By Rohit Talwar, Steve Wells, and Alexandra Whittington

How can we apply futurist thinking to enhance our responses to the current crisis and increase resilience against future shocks?

Within the futurist community there is much handwringing and frustration at the extent to which leaders, decision makers, and policy advisors have ignored past advice on global health risks and failed to respond adequately to countless preparedness studies for governments, businesses, and civil society. Since the 1960s the stock in trade of much futurist work has been to advise on both the range of risks on the horizon and also, more importantly, the response strategies to mitigate the impacts and aftereffects. From health pandemics and extreme weather events through to infrastructure shocks and financial fault lines—there has been no shortage of foresight and preparedness advice.

So, what lessons can we learn from the past and apply to both our current pandemic responses and our future scenarios? Here are ten messages that we believe need to be factored in by governments, businesses, and civil society:

1. Genuinely Global Response Mechanisms

Futurists have long since argued the centrality of coordinated international action to address many of our biggest global issues—as articulated well in the Millennium Project's 15 Global Challenges. For example, recovery from the global financial crisis is attributed in part to well-coordinated international action. In contrast, the failure to make the desired progress on climate change is blamed on weaknesses in the global policy and response mechanisms currently in place.

The current pandemic has focused attention on the fact that this is an "aircraft borne" disease that happily crosses national boundaries in seat 23B. Hence, it remains a risk for all until it has truly been brought under control everywhere, or until we ban all international flights, rail travel, and shipping—which for many would be an unthinkable option. The solutions for these global health, humanitarian, and economic crises will require coordinated and consistently executed action across the planet. From testing, treatment, and vaccination through to economic and social recovery, nations will need to work together to address the current challenges and ensure more robust future anticipatory and response mechanisms.

2. Develop Scenarios for a Range of Shocks

While many governments and central banks are modeling possible economic scenarios, they don't seem to be taking enough account of future risks and the possible phases of behavior of organizations and individuals over the next few years. The pandemic has highlighted the importance of developing scenarios for a range of possible categories of shock from health emergencies and weather disasters to terror incidents and infrastructure breakdown.

Scenarios cannot possibly cover every risk, but the broad types of underlying impact can be addressed to help inform preparedness strategies and plans. These risk and shock scenarios should either include or drive a subsequent set of scenarios which focus on the possible social and economic impacts and their aftermath. Thinking the unthinkable on a regular basis should become part of the training of every leader and manager and embedded in the governance processes of every organization—public and private.

3. Strategies, Plans, and Testing: Focus on Broad Categories of Impact

A follow-up action is to develop strategies and plans and test them against a range of the underlying scenarios. The aim is both to highlight where response mechanisms are robust and to identify key points of weakness or omission. The testing needs to start with an intellectual "**red teaming**" exercise to assess robustness, followed by a live rehearsal involving all the agencies and resources to see what happens when strategies and plans meet reality.

We cannot plan for every possible event, but we can prepare for the types of impact—be that a health crisis that impacts the whole country, or an accidental or deliberate failure that disables critical transport, communications, or utilities infrastructures. So, for example, we don't need to know all the possible causes to plan for situations where large numbers of businesses are unable to operate with the resultant impacts on the workforce.

Knowing that such events might happen allows governments to think through and put in place the responses mechanisms, such as the ability to make payments to every business and individual. Such an approach would, for example, allow alternative models of guaranteed basic income and service provision to be evaluated and appropriate delivery mechanisms to be established in advance of their need. These may never be needed but having them ready and tested means they can be mobilized rapidly. Much of what has been rushed through around the world in the midst of the current crisis would fall under this category of inevitable surprises.

4. Assume Emergency Powers Will be Required

Many governments have rushed through emergency powers to allow them to maintain public order and address the crisis. The speed of implementation leaves little time for the normal mechanisms of scrutiny by politicians, civil society organizations, the media, and the public. A more forward-looking approach would be to draft, debate, and agree such measures in advance of any emergency and then simply enact the already approved measures during the crisis. Clearly, not every eventuality can be covered—but most can.

5. Increase Resilience: Distribute Capability and Resource

The current crisis has highlighted the challenges of trying to do everything centrally in the middle of a crisis—from virus testing through to distribution of personal protective equipment (PPE). Countless preparedness exercises have highlighted the importance of having people and physical resources distributed across the nation to ensure action can be enabled quickly. At the simplest level, this means ensuring medical facilities have sufficient stocks of equipment to last them three months or more and everyone involved already knows exactly what to do in the absence of central guidance.

6. Enable Self-Organizing Systems and Networks

The crisis shows the innovative power and impact of self-organizing systems. These range from the recruitment and mobilization of thousands of volunteers and new cross-sectoral collaborations, through to solution hackathons and global data and computing capability sharing initiatives. Again, we cannot predict the exact nature of a crisis, but we can expect that self-organizing systems will be an essential part of the solution. The speed with which such initiatives can get going can be accelerated by putting in place enabling mechanisms in advance to support network conveners and coordinators.

7. Mobilize at the Earliest Warning Signals

The current crisis has highlighted huge differences in the approaches taken by different governments. Interestingly, those with some of the most sophisticated horizon scanning and risk planning mechanisms such as Singapore were able to act quickly and comprehensively. Key actions taken by such countries included closing transit borders with affected regions, implementing rapid and widespread testing and contact tracing, resourcing medical facilities, ordering additional medical supplies and equipment, and contacting retired and reservist personnel to alert them that they might be needed.

Across every broad category of risk from health to the environment, there are equivalent measures that can be taken early and pre-emptively. Clearly, there is a cost involved in maintaining higher stock levels and having fully trained personnel waiting in reserve. However, that cost is significantly lower than that now being experienced by those who are trying to resource such requirements at the same time as everyone else and in a more chaotic and uncoordinated way. The cost in human terms of unnecessary viral exposure is incalculable.

8. Explain the Underlying Science, Models, Assumptions, and Plans–Repeatedly

People crave information. Authoritative government communications help dispel misinformation and rumor and enable organizations and individuals to plan. For example, some governments have been exceptionally clear on the models they are using and the assumptions they are making. They have also been clear on how long they expect things to last, response mechanisms, and subsequent steps to end lockdowns. Of course, there are caveats because no one knows for sure how long any crisis might last.

Hence, it is crucially important to clarify whether you are anticipating a two-week disruption or a six-month one. This helps businesses to plan more effectively and enables firms and individuals to assess the potential financial impacts and act accordingly. People are far more willing to forgive timeline changes from a government that communicates clearly, than one that has obfuscated, presented mixed messages, and hedged its bets. Official, comprehensive, and regularly updated websites are critical to ensuring people are drawing from a single source of government information and advice.

9. Minimize the Crisis Agenda

The actions outlined above all help ensure better forward planning, greater resilience, and a faster speed of response. Critically, they allow governments to build public confidence and support by allowing rapid and coordinated action. They also minimize the range of crisis specific actions and decisions that need to be made at speed in the midst of a crisis. This in turn reduces the risk of poorly thought through, uncoordinated, and badly communicated crisis response measures.

10. Learning and After Action Review

However well governments address the actions outlined above, not everything will work perfectly; unexpected and unpredictable issues will still arise, and previously tested systems will fail in unanticipated ways. Hence, a willingness to acknowledge, share, and learn from these issues and mistakes is essential. These can help both in real time to refine current response strategies and in the updating of plans for future emergencies. Once the crisis has passed, a more rigorous "after action review" is vital—taking inputs from across society. This can only help improve future strategies, plans, and overall resilience.

The crisis highlighted the flawed nature of some nations' response strategies and resilience plans. This need not be the case. Not every crisis can be anticipated, but the impacts of most can be prepared for with well-constructed scenarios, robust strategies, and regularly tested and well-resourced plans. Globally, there are many people involved in foresight, future studies, risk anticipation, horizon scanning, scenario planning, and other futurist activities. Now, might be a good time to start asking for their input and acting on it.

- *What use does your government or organization make of scenario planning and horizon scanning to prepare for possible future shocks, crises, and dramatic economic disruptions?*
- *How robust are your policies, strategies, and disaster preparedness plans against the range of scenarios that might play out at the global, national, and local level?*
- *How open is your government or organization to hearing difficult messages and considering previously unthinkable scenarios that could overturn your current assumptions, policies, and plans?*

More Aware, More Agile, More Alive

By David W. Wood

Why have risks of major crises, such as a worldwide pandemic, been poorly handled and how can a global risk management system emerge to manage future, nastier, more potentially impactful risks more effectively?

Following the wake-up call of the recent pandemic, I believe a new world is possible. It's a world that is more aware, more agile, and more alive. Such a world is not just possible, it's highly desirable. Whether this kind of global transition takes place over the coming years will determine if the longer-term future for humanity is dismal or glorious.

Changes Afoot

One of the routes out of the crisis is seen to be the embrace of developments in science and technology. Titanic forces of change are already afoot here. Revolutions are gathering pace in four overlapping fields of technology: nanotech, biotech, infotech, and cognotech (NBIC). These NBIC revolutions are following the same accelerating curve that the recent pandemic has made all-too-familiar: a period of slow, local change morphs into a period of faster, larger change—and then into a period of even faster, world-encompassing disruption.

New technologies bring new possibilities. Altered sets of alliances and rivalries are reshaping the fields of international commerce and even international politics. The greater the pace of change, the more intense the dislocation. Due to the increased scale and speed of these ongoing technology revolutions, the disruptions that followed in the wake of previous industrial revolutions—traumatic though they were—could be dwarfed in comparison to what lies ahead.

Humanity now faces some hard but critical choices—with decisions that will determine our future. If we choose poorly, technology will do much more harm than good. Instead of the flourishing of the "better angels of our human nature," it will be our inner demons that technology magnifies. But if we are truly aware—and truly agile—then humanity can become truly alive, for the first time in history, reaching new levels of collaboration, creativity, compassion, and consciousness.

Hindering Awareness

Let's recall what happened after another recent global crisis. I'm referring, not to the current case of biological contagion, but to the financial contagion of the global financial crisis of 2008. Shortly afterwards, Queen Elizabeth was invited to open a new building at the London School of Economics. In front of a large crowd of distinguished economists, she asked why no one had predicted the crisis. After a delay, a group of professors wrote to the Queen.[25] Their answers have important lessons for us now in 2020, just as much as when the letter was first written. They identified three issues:

1. A "feel-good factor" which "masked how out-of-kilter the world economy had become beneath the surface"
2. A "psychology of denial" that "gripped the financial and political world"
3. An over-trust in "financial wizards" who "managed to convince themselves and the world's politicians that they had found clever ways to spread risk throughout financial markets."

My hope for what comes out of the current crisis will be a clearer, more sober understanding of the precariousness and uncertainty of the future wellbeing of humanity. We cannot let ourselves be misled by feel-good factors, pleasant though they are, the psychology of denial, reassuring though that seems, or over-trust in smooth-talking leaders and financial wizards.

Consider Exercise Cygnus, carried out by the UK government in the latter months of 2016. This vividly highlighted the lack of preparedness in the UK for a possible future pandemic. Government ministers were reportedly left "ashen-faced" in horror.[26] But then … nothing much changed. Feel-good factors prevailed. A psychology of denial frustrated plans to act responsibly on the alarming lessons of the exercise. Therefore, the UK sleepwalked into the pandemic debacle—despite astute warnings from forecasters such as Bill Gates.[27]

Why Risks Lack Attention

Lack of preparation for the recent pandemic is as nothing compared to society's lack of preparation for even nastier, tougher risks that await in the near future. What contingencies are in place to address pathogens deliberately engineered to be more deadly, infections of computer malware that cripple the global infrastructure, and aberrant combinations of faulty artificial intelligence software and megaton nuclear weaponry?

I see five key reasons for our lack of preparedness:

1. Failure to comprehend the compounding nature of exponential growth
2. Our overoptimism bias, perhaps because optimists are generally more successful in life than pessimists
3. Our short-term bias, including five-year election cycles and quarterly business reports
4. Apprehension that risk mitigation would slow down technology progress that has many other benefits
5. The fact that risk mitigation is a public good: benefits apply to everyone, but each individual is loath to bear the cost alone.

In response, I would argue that we need:

1. Better education about exponential change—including the factors that cause it to slow and stop, as well as the factors that cause it to explode
2. Improved skills in constructive pessimism—psychologically informed communications
3. Advocates for the future—including the approach taken by some countries of appointing a government minister with full-time responsibility in this area
4. The development of a risk management framework which combines foresight with contingency planning and properly resourced and regularly tested rapid response capabilities
5. The intervention of government, to fund work in these areas that no individual company is willing to undertake.

A major complication with the last two points is the international nature of the issues involved. Risk mitigation is a public good at the global level as well as the national one. Likewise, no single country in a technological arms race wants to be left behind rivals that play faster and looser with safety norms.

Consequently, our awareness and agility need to be elevated from national to global levels. Just as the catastrophe of World War Two led to the prudent creation of the UN and various international Bretton Woods organizations, so too can the current crisis lead to the emergence or revitalization of global bodies to anticipate and manage risks. Who will show the leadership to drive the creation of these new era institutions and mechanisms?

Boosting Agility

I'll close by highlighting what I see as four vital aspects of the global risk management framework,[28] to help boost future agility:

1. Regular horizon scanning and scenario analysis in advance, drawing on insights from multiple disciplines and diverse perspectives
2. Constant monitoring, for any developments different from what was forecast or encompassed by those scans and scenarios

3. A spirit of openness and transparency, that values data over ideology, and transcends tribal instincts

4. Effective, vivid, and credible communications to maintain and engage public support.

- *Which single factor is the most important in preventing society from being properly aware of forthcoming risks of major humanitarian setbacks?*
- *Which single factor is the most important in preventing society from being able to respond in a powerful and agile way to future possible humanitarian setbacks?*
- *What is the most likely way to establish a framework for effective international cooperation in the face of potential major humanitarian setbacks?*

David Wood is a smartphone industry pioneer, Symbian co-founder, chair of London Futurists, principal of Delta Wisdom, singularitarian, transhumanist, and executive director of Transpolitica. David has a background in mathematics and the philosophy of science. He is the author or lead editor of nine books, including RAFT 2035, Smartphones and Beyond, The Abolition of Aging, Sustainable Superabundance, and Transcending Politics. davidw@deltawisdom.com

Using the Crisis to Remake Government for the Future

By Geoff Mulgan

How might governments' innovative pandemic responses point to the possibility of radically different approaches in the future, from data to mental health and civic mobilization to transparency?

The pandemic could be just a one-off blip, with normal service resuming once the worst of it is over. But it could be used to accelerate changes that were long overdue. Here I look at what might happen to government once the crisis is over, and how some of the actions may point to a radically different vision of future government.

Openness and Many Models

The story of this crisis confirms what we should already know: the vital importance of free flows of information. This was confirmed by China's disastrous early moves such as denial and attacking whistle-blowers. In overly hierarchical and authoritarian governments, there are too many incentives to cover up uncomfortable facts. Hopefully China and other countries will remember the vital importance of independent statistical agencies and free flows of data.

Taiwan has been a particularly good example of radical transparency,[29] combining bottom-up civic creativity and technocratic efficiency. Many others have gone a long way in opening up their analysis, data, models, and reasoning so that they can be critiqued and improved. The crucial lesson is that we often need more and better models, and more interrogation of models, rather than fetishizing any single model, as some governments and media commentary have done. Indeed, the opening up of models to scrutiny could point to a future where many aspects of government are informed by open and competing models, and visible learning when they turn out to be right or wrong.

Data

The crisis highlighted the new tools available to governments to observe, monitor, and predict. The most impressive examples have included Singapore's contact tracking methods, South Korea's massive testing program underpinned by data, and the use of mobile phone and travel data across East Asia. Seoul's use and sharing of data is particularly remarkable with, still, zero deaths in a city of 11 million.

Although many of these methods raise questions about civil liberties, they also point to what could become possible around climate change and other challenges. The conventional reaction against these—which only emphasizes individual privacy—could look anachronistic. Instead attention will hopefully shift to the arrangements needed to govern data and data-sharing in the public interest.

Collective Intelligence

There has been an extraordinary upsurge of collective intelligence responses[30] and crowdsourcing new technologies, treatments, and policies at a global scale. These are accelerating the spread of what I call **intelligence assemblies** within nations—pulling together data of all kinds, citizen insights—and which could become the spine of almost every aspect of government in the future.

Agile Communication

The crisis has seen the adoption of a wide range of classic information strategies, with lengthy speeches by presidents and prime ministers laying down the new rules. The best have been upfront about the risks, open with the facts, and honest about the uncertainties. There has also been a lot of experimentation with WhatsApp, chatbots of all kinds, and local groups. The aim has been to help people make sense of their own risks and symptoms. For the first time, we have also seen serious action on the part of the big platforms to deal with rampant lies and misinformation, as they realize that they have become de facto public services. This might be one of the better legacies of the crisis.

Anticipation

The crisis is showing the potential power of anticipatory governance. In Singapore, for example, 40% of those tested were contacted by the government rather than self-presenting, because contact data showed they had been close to infected people. There are many other fields where government could operate in much more anticipatory ways. For example, using data and SMS as proactive tools, spotting and preventing problems rather than only curing them, whether in education, health, or welfare.

Civic Mobilization

Everywhere we are seeing an extraordinary mobilization of societies to look after the isolated and elderly. The UK, for example, has mobilized 750,000 volunteers for the health service, using the <u>GoodSam app</u> (developed by Nesta). Other examples like RallyRound use platform technologies to orchestrate circles of support for those in need. These point to what should be being done anyway, as societies face epidemics of loneliness and the need for radical overhauls of care systems that can't only rely on paid professionals.

Welfare

The extraordinary moves to put in place income support for individuals, and cash support for businesses, point to a very different possible future for government. For example, some countries already have single accounts for businesses and citizens, which, in principle, make it much easier to loan money on different terms, or to introduce new universal basic income (UBI) type schemes. Examples would include Singapore's MyInfo and Central Addressing System, India's Aadhaar, and Nemkonto in Denmark. The absence of anything like these mechanisms has greatly hampered action in some countries.

Mental Health

Large-scale isolation puts a big pressure on mental health and can manifest itself in the form of domestic violence, depression, anxiety, and particular challenges for young men. Governments in the past have only concerned themselves with the most acute cases—but population level mental health is fast becoming a policy concern (not least because of growing evidence on how different interventions can have an impact). The work of organizations like Action for Happiness, with strongly evidenced interventions to improve everyday mental health, could be further integrated into public policy.

We should never waste a crisis. An incredible amount of thought, creativity, and commitment is going into the responses around us right now. Hopefully some of these will be used to remake government in ways that make it better suited to the challenges that lie ahead.

- *How would you assess governments' ability and willingness to learn from each other about future responses to disruptive global events?*
- *What role would you anticipate society more broadly playing in the decision-making process in response to future global disruption?*
- *How might the societal response to the pandemic help to enable a more human future?*

Geoff Mulgan is professor of Collective Intelligence, Public Policy and Social Innovation at University College London. He was CEO of Nesta, director of Demos and the Young Foundation, director of the UK Government's Strategy Unit, and head of policy in the UK Prime Minister's office. His books include Big Mind (Princeton) and Social Innovation (Policy Press). geoff.mulgan@gmail.com

The Great Separation

By Bronwyn Williams

Will 2020 be a great equalizer or a great divider?

The global economic crisis brought on by the pandemic of 2019 is by no means an equalizing crisis. Indeed, one of the most significant lasting socio-economic effects of the crisis will be the likely opening up of the fault lines running underneath fragile modern society. Specifically, the fault lines between rich and poor, young and old, and the welfare state itself.

The center may not hold.

The Winner Takes All

Protracted lockdowns the world over have resulted in widespread economic destruction and wholesale unemployment. Despite all the government and central bank bailout and assistance packages to plug the economic holes, there is still a significant segment of the economy that falls into unaddressed gaps.

After decades of low wage growth compared to labor productivity growth, the global middle class is already fragile. Now, a deep economic shock could well see the survival of only the financially fittest. The result—the rich get richer, the poor get poorer, as only the richest individuals hold enough savings to fall back on. Similarly, only the biggest, most well-funded businesses would have the reserves to survive the coming months.

At the individual level, the so-called "missing middle," also known as the precariat, or the precarious proletariat class, is particularly affected. This large segment of the lower-income tranches of the middle class is made up of freelancers, non-essential gig workers, and micro-entrepreneurs with unpredictable and insecure incomes. These workers perform tasks and provide services that cannot easily transition online. As such, they find themselves without any income at all for the duration of lockdown periods.

The poorest, most vulnerable workers have the least resources to cushion themselves against the huge economic shock, and they are the most likely to lose their jobs and income. Even worse, this segment of the market was typically not covered by government-sponsored wage subsidies and their businesses may have been too small to qualify for big bailout money. Hence, this group, particularly in developing nations, is at risk of falling below the poverty line, into economic hardship, or reliance on state welfare in more fortunate economies.

Notably, as Benjamin Franklin said, "When there is no middle class, there can be no democracy." What he meant is that societies can hardly be considered democratic at all where workers do not have a stake in the financial rewards or upside of their own economies and their own contribution to that economy. A strong, financially independent middle class is essential for democracy and social stability.

At a business level, small to medium sized enterprises (SMEs) typically have much shorter cash runways and much less access to emergency credit than their larger counterparts. Furthermore, even the businesses that do survive the immediate economic shutdown period have to expect a long, slow recovery period ahead after lockdown lifts. This means preparing for months, if not years, of lower profits and fewer cash-flush customers in a generally economically depressed environment. Only the biggest and best funded businesses are likely to survive.

The more that SMEs fail, the more that bigger businesses win, as these better resourced survivors are able to take back market share and customers from their smaller competitors. This further enhances the effect of vicious circles for the smaller, poorer, and weaker and virtuous circles for the bigger, richer, and stronger.

At an international level, poorer countries in developing markets across "the Global South" simply do not have the fiscal reserves to support their affected citizens and businesses in the same way that richer nations are able to. Among the poorest, most vulnerable communities on earth, there are no helicopter payments or bailout packages forthcoming to ease their suffering. Indeed, many emerging market governments will find themselves competing for International Monetary Fund (IMF) and BRICs bank loans to keep their populations fed. This of course will only increase the indebtedness of these nations and widen the gap between developed and developing countries and their respective citizens.

The end result is that the twin health and economic crises of the 2020s will likely deepen the rich–poor divide, both between international economies, and within national populations. This, in turn will serve to change and destabilize international relationship power dynamics, depending on which nations get funding and from what sources. It seems increasingly likely that funding for many African nations, for example, will come from the east rather than the west, indicating a power switch away from dollar hegemony lies ahead.

All this adds fuel to already-simmering tensions around growing intra-country and international global inequality.

Intergenerational Conflict

The impact of the twin 2020's health and financial crises has also magnified pre-existing conflicts between the various generational cohorts competing for each nation's resources. To put it bluntly, while elderly people were dying on ventilators in the intensive care units, young people were seen partying on beaches for spring break.

In more concrete terms, an uncomfortable truth is that while the benefits of social distancing and lockdowns serve to protect the health of the elderly and physically vulnerable in society, these were the demographics seen as most likely to suffer complications from contracting the virus. However, it is the younger generations who seem likely to bear the brunt of the short- and long-term economic fallout.

As part of society's dependent population, older people living off pensions or state welfare no longer need to work to earn a living. Younger workers, however, must earn an income to survive, and it is they that find themselves unemployed and without savings to fall back on. These younger generations will also have to pay for the bailouts and stimulus packages in the form of excess tax burdens, reductions in public services, and, in all likelihood, inflation, as the effects of monetary stimulus packages slowly make their way into market pricing models, over the coming years and decades.

This economic reality also highlights the fragility and limitations of the social security welfare safety net systems that rely on young, growing populations to fund the benefits of older generations. That social contract breaks down when younger generations realize they will not receive the same value of social welfare benefits in their own old age that they are currently funding for older generations. As the young begin to feel short-changed by their forbearers, they could rebel against the idea of paying into tax-funded pension and medical aid schemes from which they are unlikely to benefit.

Already we can see the signs of the intergenerational divide growing. Younger political activists around the world are lobbying both to lower minimum voting ages and implement maximum voting ages to reduce the political power of older demographics in their democracies.

The New Social Contract?

In short, the 2020's crises are likely to deepen the divide between old and young, rich and poor, individuals and nations. Opening up these fault lines could destabilize the socio-economic contracts of both capitalist and social democratic nations, with as yet unknown consequences.

For this reason, perhaps the best name for this period in time should be the Great Separation.

- *Can democracy survive the fracture of the fragile middle class?*
- *What would happen if the social security contract between generations breaks down in your country?*

- *How can we build bridges between social divides to secure the resilience of our societies?*

Bronwyn Williams is a futurist, economist, and trend analyst. She is currently a partner at Flux Trends and Apollo42. In addition to her foresight work, Bronwyn is also a keynote speaker and a regular media commentator on socio-economic trends. bronwyn@fluxtrends.co.za

Which Way America? Four Alternative Futures

By Leland A. Shupp

What are some possible outcomes for the US in the next 3-5 years?

The US plays a pivotal role in the global economy and international institutions, but its future is highly uncertain, depending on the shape of economic recovery and outcome of the coming election. What different outcomes are possible over the next 3-5 years?

We live in a strange and surreal time. As we go to press in May 2020, a global pandemic is spreading, with over five million people infected and more than 300,000 deaths worldwide. This has hit the US especially hard, as I believe the lack of a coordinated and informed national response has cost thousands of lives and billions of dollars.

Apologies to my international friends for the US focus, but I believe the US is at the tip of the spear for key economic and political trends. We have both the largest global economy and arguably the most unpredictable leader, whose decisions have global impact.

The highest levels of uncertainty for the US appear to be in the nature of the economic recovery and who will be the next President of the US—incumbent Republican Donald Trump or Democratic nominee Joe Biden. Given those variables, here I explore four alternative possible futures for the US in 2024.

Scenario 1: The American Reich

Characteristics: V-shaped economic recovery; Trump re-elected

In this scenario, we see a steep economic decline followed by a fast and robust economic recovery, surprising almost everyone. Epidemiologists discover that much of the US population already had antibodies to the virus, suggesting that the virus was more widespread and less lethal than previously estimated. Assuming the population was nearing herd immunity levels, travel restrictions were lifted, and commerce resumed quickly. Breathing a collective sigh of relief, businesses began rehiring and growing quickly to meet pent-up demand.

Trump claimed credit for the rapid recovery, boasting he knew the threat wasn't that serious all along. Republicans engineered a second Trump presidency with help from Russian and right-wing disinformation campaigns and voter suppression. The second Trump term is a disaster for democracy, as democratic institutions are attacked with renewed vigor and utter disregard for prior norms.

By packing the judiciary (with a solid Supreme Court majority), gerrymandering districts, and voter suppression, the Republican Party entrenches itself. It becomes a state party that attacks all opposition, crushing dissent as disloyalty. Fox News becomes the official US media outlet. As the 2024 election nears, Presidential term limits are eliminated, and Republicans have effectively established an American Reich.

Scenario 2: Renewal

Characteristics: U-shaped economic recovery; Biden elected

In this scenario, we see slower and more gradual economic recovery with Trump blamed for his incompetence in managing the crisis. There was also a growing realization that strong government institutions were needed to prevent future crises. It becomes apparent that a coordinated and prompt national pandemic response could have saved many lives and much economic pain.

With the economy barely beginning to recover, Trump lost in a landslide. Democrats built a bigger majority in the House and won a Senate majority. With Democrats back in control, rebuilding of government institutions began, and there was a renewed emphasis on government as a source of expertise and services. A national healthcare plan was passed, as the virus demonstrated the importance of keeping everyone healthy, not just the wealthy and the employed.

America began to re-engage globally but found that it was no longer automatically granted a leadership role, as burned bridges take time to rebuild. The US became more a partner than dominant leader in global institutions. Headed into the 2024 election, Democrats get credit for the recovery and have momentum with a platform of strong government, healthcare for all, and renewed global engagement.

Scenario 3: Rough Sledding

Characteristics: W-shaped economic recovery; Biden elected

In this scenario, we see stops and starts as the economy reopened gradually, and increased human contact caused spikes in infection rates, leading to more movement restrictions. It became apparent that the lack of a coordinated national response was costing lives and strangling the economy, as different states loosened restrictions, only to tighten them as the virus returned in more virulent form.

Democrats won the presidency and increased their House majority, but the Senate remained in Republican control. Biden used his executive powers to rebuild federal agencies and to coordinate a national response to the pandemic, but he faced entrenched opposition from the Senate. An active right-wing resistance took hold, encouraged by Republican leadership opposed to increasing governmental control.

These oppositional forces reinforce the start and stop impact on the recovery, as a gridlocked and dysfunctional national government focused more on infighting than on pragmatic and proven policy. The 2024 election is up for grabs, as the Democratic platform of strong government and international engagement is unable to demonstrate fast results, and a Republican resurgence based on opposition to big government and elite expertise gains momentum.

Scenario 4: The Greatest Depression

Characteristics: L-shaped economic recovery; Biden elected

In this scenario, a prolonged depression results in the US experiencing little economic recovery, with a downward spiral of jobs, shrinking companies, and consumer spending. The cost of inaction at the onset of the crisis became starkly apparent, with a shrinking economy, layoffs, bankruptcies, and drastically reduced consumer spending reinforcing each other. New strains of the virus appeared in more deadly forms, staying ahead of testing and vaccination efforts.

Biden won the presidency and Democrats won the House, but not the Senate. He used executive powers to rebuild federal agencies and coordinate a national pandemic response, but faced entrenched opposition from the Senate and an increasingly restless and scared public demanding immediate relief.

An active right-wing resistance grew into armed opposition in some states, and the Republican Party became even more radicalized. A charismatic new Republican leader emerges - a smarter, more charismatic version of Trump, and a grassroots isolationist, anti-government, and survivalist movement arises, building an underground resistance and gaining momentum leading up to the 2024 elections.

- *When developing scenarios do you focus on identifying the most likely scenario, or embrace the ideas of equal plausibility?*
- *What are the critical enablers for the development of strategy that may work across a number of different scenarios?*
- *How do you create effective strategies when scenarios suggest radically different plausible futures?*

Leland A. Shupp has been helping companies identify new growth opportunities for products, services, and brands for 20+ years. He integrates customer insights with foresight, design thinking, and advanced analytics to help companies grow and prosper. foresightSF@gmail.com

Reshaping the Economic Agenda

By Rohit Talwar, Steve Wells, and Alexandra Whittington

What factors should sit at the heart of national economic recovery plans to lay a foundation for a more sustainable and viable future for all citizens?

The pandemic is now truly global—having spread to 212 countries and territories around the world. While some countries like New Zealand have declared an end to the crisis and others like Germany, Spain, Italy, and the US have started to ease lockdown conditions, others are extending theirs or refusing to commit to an exit strategy. Globally, concerns are mounting over the depth of social impact. Unemployment for some countries is rising to levels higher than in the Great Depression and dire warnings are being issued on the global economic outlook. Here in the UK, the government's Office for Budget Responsibility is warning that the economy could shrink by 35% by June.

In the midst of an unending stream of bleak news, countries are also having to think about the mechanics of recovery. Many are wrestling with the issue of how they can balance addressing an immense agenda of short-term priorities with the need to ensure a path to a sustainable and viable medium- to long-term future. Here, we examine five critical economic policy areas in which robust, bold, and innovative thinking will be required to map a path forward on societal grand challenges.

1. Country Viability

Prior to the pandemic, many countries were already in economic and social intensive care. Some nations will inevitably be pushed to or over the brink. They simply cannot fund the combination of the health and social costs of dealing with the situation, coupled with the bill for economic support to businesses, individuals, and financial markets. This is being further exacerbated by the loss of tax revenues, declining foreign earnings, the level of business failures, and the growth in long-term unemployment. With the potential for second and third waves of business closures and job losses once economic activity picks back up, this could push more countries into economic distress.

Richer nations may coalesce around institutions such as the World Bank, IMF, and OECD to try and effect bailouts for some badly affected countries. However, for some, there may be no viable future as independent nations. Tough choices may be required about whether they seek to merge, come under another nation's patronage or sponsorship, or effectively be taken over by others with better governance, operational capacity, infrastructure, and resources.

2. The Social Fabric

Governments will need to think hard about the goals for society in a post-pandemic world and the economic and social actions required to get there. Across the globe, society is feeling the impacts in different ways. Some people are clearly finding new levels of inner peace and purpose with a calmer, less disrupted pattern to daily life. However, for others we see a rise in problems associated with underemployment, unemployment, and confinement, such as mental health issues and domestic violence.

The economic aspects of the generational divide could also become a critical focus of policy making. Could the lockdown exit strategies further reinforce tensions, with the young and healthy being given preference over the old, the infirm, and those with complex health conditions? Will younger generations oppose paying into public pension schemes from which they will not benefit for decades—if at all?

Some countries may opt to drive the retirement age up or down to address the short-term challenges, while also seeking innovative new solutions for how to fulfill their pension responsibilities going forward. Finally, some may also look to accelerate advances in the field of human augmentation to effectively engineer more resilient and disease resistant humans to enable more people to work later in life and thus reduce their dependency on the state.

The outcomes, organization, and economics of health and care systems will also need to be reimagined, drawing on the lessons of the pandemic. In the short term, once the crisis starts to subside, an already frazzled health sector will be hit with a wave of pent-up demand from those whose consultations, diagnostic tests, and treatments had been put on hold.

The new design will need to think about how to fund enlarged public expectations and address the obvious differences in access and outcomes being revealed by the pandemic. For example, in the UK black and Asian people were found to be four times more likely to die of the virus than their white counterparts. The reimagined system will also need to engineer in greater flexibility, have the capacity to mobilize testing for future diseases, and develop strategies to enhance wellbeing and encourage the population to use data, science, and technology to improve self-care.

Education systems may also never be the same again. The economics of education funding will be under scrutiny and governments are likely to face intense pressure to raise the priority placed on education as a cornerstone of future economic growth and sustainability. Well-resourced education systems and institutions generally adapted well to electronic delivery. They were able to continue delivering lessons and enabling learning in the digital realm. Many could emerge with far richer models that blend the physical and digital learning domains more effectively. This will also be enabled by the rapid improvement in digital literacy for many teachers and parents.

However, for those less well resourced, the process of catching up on missed months of learning could create major challenges. Furthermore, the lack of resources could leave them just as exposed should more lockdowns be required. These factors could have adverse knock-on effects on pupils' education, public examination results, and access to higher education for some time to come. This could indeed deepen educational divides across socio-economic groups and within and between towns, cities, and countries.

3. Incomes and Unemployment

Despite the media noise, in practice no country has implemented an unconditional basic income (UBI). Instead, a complex mix of temporary payments, minimum incomes, payment of furloughed workers, loans, and a variety of other mechanisms have been implemented. The issue of what to do next is put into sharp focus by the steep rises in unemployment globally, coupled with the potential for further job losses through business failures and automation.

At present the debate continues to rage over whether a UBI is politically and socially desirable, how it can be funded, whether it makes sense to pay it to those who don't need it, and the potential impact on people's willingness to work. With a prolonged recession or depression on the cards for many nations, and indeed the entire planet, the need to think about UBI and other alternatives is already on the agenda and will be rising up it fast.

4. The Business Ecosystem

Governments will need to plan for a range of scenarios around business failure and the resulting employment impacts. Many of the clear potential winners and losers at the sectoral level have been discussed elsewhere. The challenge is understanding the possible scenarios for that middle ground of businesses that have effectively been put on hold for now—in sectors ranging from hotels and aviation to luxury goods, entertainment, and dining. As yet, the number of clear business failures has been relatively limited. However, the longer the lockdowns continue and the slower the exit process, the more the viability of some or many of these firms will be called into question.

Furthermore, even when the recovery starts, business revenues may not return to pre-crisis levels for many—particularly given increased unemployment and uncertainty on the part of those still in jobs. Hence, government planning has to prepare for several possibilities—starting with an immediate wave of business closures once lockdowns end. This will likely be followed by a second wave of failures as spending levels become clearer in the months after lockdown and the startups that look the least promising in the new post-pandemic order fail to secure follow-on funding. These could then drive further successive waves of closures as the impacts ripple through supply chains.

Of course, these failures need to be set against the potential for job creation by those who see the opportunity to start new ventures. Downturns provide an environment where investment capital may be cheaper, and a range of government incentives may be on offer to start a business. The issue will be around the potential skills mismatch between the needs of these new ventures and those of the people losing their jobs in failing and shrinking businesses.

The drastic hit to revenues that many businesses are taking now will inevitably impact their targets and budgets for the current financial year. A poor current financial year will in turn drive spending budgets for the following financial year. Hence, the knock-on impacts for business spending will again hit firms further down the value chain. The pain will be unevenly spread. For example, we can expect to see higher levels of investment in process automation and artificial intelligence as firms seek to increase their ability to continue operating irrespective of potential future pandemic impacts on their workforce.

5. National Economic Development Plans

The last few years have seen many developed and developing nations alike from the Middle East and Africa through to Asia and Latin America laying out bold visions for the future. These range in scope from 2025 to 2050 and many contain blueprints for the type of society, economy, and industry sectors they want to evolve. The crisis has put a lot of that thinking on hold. However, the same bold thinking and imagination will be required to map a slightly different path to the future—and to potentially accelerate ideas that were previously considered a decade or more away.

We believe these plans now need to address three separate time-frames and their associated challenges:

The next two years—This is about the recovery plan, building resilience, and reducing exposure to future shocks. In a world of disrupted supply chains, the old logic of industry specialization and import reliance may come under challenge. Hence many nations may look to become more self-sufficient and build up their own capabilities across the entire gamut of products and services they might previously have sourced from overseas. This means building small footprint factories using the latest technologies and looking to accelerate industrial scale use of techniques such as 3D printing.

This will also be a period of accelerated capacity building and developing skills across the board for both the public and private sector. Competition for the best talent globally will also increase as nations seek to build local expertise centers in areas ranging from rapid construction and vertical farming to synthetic biology and new materials. New partnerships will be required with IP owners and expertise centers around the world. At the same time, many manufacturers may be looking to contract their geographic footprint. Hence, they may be happy to enter into such IP focused arrangements which reduce their reliance on having to manufacture in uncertain times.

The next three to five years—Here the focus should be on building from the foundations laid in the previous two years. Turning the research and development (R&D) investments and capacity building into viable businesses that create local jobs and drive the economy. Done well, this will allow greater focus on investment in the next wave of R&D that will drive the following decade of economic development. This needs to happen in parallel with initiating deep transformation of lifelong education systems and establishing new civil society infrastructure and governance mechanisms. While the actions may not start for two or more years, planning for them and laying the foundations needs to start alongside the near-term recovery actions.

The next six to ten years or more—This is the period in which many of the most promising ideas in science and technology could bring about transformative developments. The possibilities are immense and mind-blowing, ranging from Hyperloop transport systems to driverless vehicles. Deep societal transformations could also be enabled by truly artificially intelligent systems and the engineering of more robust and disease resistant humans. These developments do not move at a linear pace and some nations are keen to make them happen on a faster timescale. Hence, in the next two years, nations need to be accelerating their R&D in these fields. This will allow for capability development in the following few years that in turn will drive the commercialization of these fields in the six- to ten-year time frame—or earlier.

Many may think their plate is already full with just navigating the day to day of the current crisis. However, the crisis also provides a window in which to pursue a bold and innovative rethinking of the core mechanisms across society, the economy, and government. Now may well be the best time to start that thinking.

- *How should national economic development plans be restructured to address both the challenges emerging from the pandemic and the opportunities presented by advances in science, technology, and innovation?*
- *What priority should nations be placing on education, health and care systems, and the social fabric when laying out their post-pandemic visions and strategies?*
- *How can nations shift from globalized models of resourcing to ones where they must be more self-sufficient in providing the products and services they consume?*

BUSINESS AND TECHNOLOGY

Snapback—Don't Expect a Post-Pandemic Remote Working Boom

By Tom Cheesewright

Will working from home practices become embedded or could we see a return to pre-pandemic behaviors when the lockdown ends?

The lockdown ends. We all open our doors and breathe a collective sigh of relief that can be heard across the land. What then? Will this crisis leave an indelible mark on our behaviors? Or will things return to the way they were?

I believe there is good reason to expect a significant snapback to many of our pre-pandemic behaviors, particularly around the nature of work.

Push and Pull

Large-scale societal change requires both motivation and opportunity. The pandemic has created an artificial scenario where certain behaviors are enforced. People, who were otherwise unaware of new technologies or previously unwilling to adopt new practices, have experienced new things like remote working. The opportunity has been there for a long time—at least in theory. The pandemic provided the motivation.

There seems to be an expectation that having experienced remote working, people will both like it and carry on with it when the crisis abates. After all, there is evidence, such as this report "Does working from home work? Evidence from a Chinese experiment,"[31] which shows that people working remotely can be more productive and more committed. Lots of people, particularly in the technology industry, have been working remotely for years and they love it! So, why wouldn't everyone else want to do it?

I believe this argument ignores three fundamental issues that are very unlikely to have been addressed by the hurried switch to remote working that the pandemic brought about:

1. Lots of people don't want to work remotely
2. Lots of managers don't want their teams to work remotely
3. Most companies are not equipped to get best value from remote workers.

I Like the Office

I looked for solid statistics on the proportion of workers that want to work remotely. I found lots of surveys of those who already work remotely, praising its benefits. So, I turned my query around and started looking for data about why people like offices. I found a similarly biased marketing driven bunch of reports about why certain groups—millennials and those in high performing companies—prefer the office.

So, without the time to conduct proper research, I turned to Twitter for a completely unscientific one-day poll. A sample of 63 people responded to the following:

"Unscientific #poll time. Complete this statement: 'At the end of week one of #lockdown I .... to the office.

- Can't wait to get back
- Never want to go back'"

Thirty-seven people said they never want to go back to the office. But 26 said that they can't wait to get back. You can't read a lot into a small Twitter poll with an audience that is skewed towards my technology and business followers, and where the respondents self-selected from within this pool. Nonetheless, the results fit to some extent with my expectations.

Lots of people like working remotely. They're comfortable with the technology. They have nice spaces to work in. They have plenty of self-discipline and motivation to do it. They work for a progressive and supportive employer. They are self-sufficient when it comes to the social interactions we all require.

However, probably just as many people don't like it. They like the harder boundaries on the working day that arriving and leaving provide. They like someone else being responsible for the information technology (IT) and the infrastructure. They like getting out of their flat or house and into somewhere different. They thrive on the physical connection with their colleagues and customers. These are feelings and attitudes that may well be hardened by the enforced isolation of lockdown.

Present and Correct

Lots of CEOs understand the value of remote working in terms of productivity and overhead costs. Lots of workers want to do it. Lots of managers hate it. Several countries, such as the UK, still have a deeply embedded culture of presenteeism. The mindset here is that the people who are working hard are the ones who show up first and leave last. The ones who grind out the hours at their desks. Those people give managers confidence. Are they working hard? Absolutely: just look at them.

Managing people you can't see is harder. How do you know they're not slacking off? That they're not slumped on the sofa streaming the latest boxset?

Culture is King

The hard lesson for managers to learn is that it doesn't matter. Who cares when people work, if they are delivering? This is not an attitude that we learn in most traditional workplaces as we come up in the world of work. It is probably a part of the productivity conundrum: we don't really learn to measure and manage actual output value.

People and companies can only extract the maximum value from remote working when they accept that it is not just about transporting office behaviors to the home. If people are to work remotely then they need both responsibility and autonomy. They should be allowed to change all the things about the office that prevent them fulfilling their potential. Get up when your body clock tells you. Work at the hours of your peak performance. Take regular breaks to do something different.

If we spend the spring and summer of 2020 with lots of companies rushing into remote working programs and doing their utmost to recreate the office environment remotely, then we're going to build a huge evidence base against its effectiveness. Armies of people trying to maintain a nine to five schedule, with managers digitally peering over their shoulders will find that they don't really like working remotely. And many employers—and particularly managers—will find their attachment to the office reinforced.

Snapback

Cultural change takes time. The recent pre-pandemic growth in remote working was leading the cultural change required to make it a productive and pleasant experience—accelerating the transition by somewhere between months and years, depending on the organization. The enforced shift to remote working that the lockdown has created is just as likely to set back this trend as to accelerate it, if many people's experience is negative.

This is not to say that more remote working isn't the future: I believe it is. But we should not expect this shock to be the catalyst that causes a complete transition.

- *Do your staff and colleagues want to work remotely? Do you?*
- *Are your people equipped for remote working? Do they have the spare living space and an environment that is comfortable and safe to work in?*

- *Does your organization have the right culture and structure for remote working? A focus on results, distributed responsibility and carefully bounded autonomy?*

Tom Cheesewright is an applied futurist working with governments and global Fortune 500 companies to help them to see the future more clearly, share that vision, and respond. His second book, *Future Proof Your Business*, was published by Penguin in April 2020. tom@bookofthefuture.co.uk

Transformative Re-Structuring

By Alida Draudt

How might business practices shift to adapt to a post-pandemic world, and what transformative effects could these changes have on broader society?

When looking at the trajectory of the first three months of 2020, a striking realization occurred—it seemed to me that we were living in a pandemic reality that closely followed the Institute for the Future (IFTF) Alternative Futures model. A mainstay in futures thinking, the Alternative Futures method outlines four main archetypes (Growth, Collapse, Constraint, Transformation) that, when strung together, seemed to fit the reality experienced by a majority of pandemic-stricken American and global societies. Stable economic Growth since 2009 dissolved into a sudden and intense Collapse scenario as contamination spread and fear thrust us into a reality hard to imagine just a few weeks prior.

Rapid decline of health, economic, and social indicators forced reactions from local, state, and federal governments that led us into a necessary Constraint scenario. Shelter-in-place and quarantine rules became the new normal—forcing nearly all industries to change their operating models significantly for the benefit of larger society.

While existence within a Constraint scenario is grim, it also offers the opportunity for reconsideration. Sitting at the precipice of potential Transformation, over the next two to five years, both American and global societies could see enormous change across all spectrums of life. Perhaps none will be shifted as abruptly as the global business sector with the massive adaptations required to compete in a post-pandemic world. The following is a speculative view of what business life could be like in 2023, three years on from the 2020 pandemic.

Digitally Global

In 2023, productivity soars across industries that embraced digital tools and big technology solutions to run their basic operations during the Great Isolation and the recurring isolationist periods that followed.

Travel frugality stunts the business travel sector, with frequent travelers opting instead for connection via teleconference or mixed reality (MR). Some advanced businesses are beginning to experiment with adapting virtual reality (VR) gaming platforms to boost business engagements, offering a variety of productivity services.

While in-person engagements are still highly valued, they come at a premium and the one-meeting business trip has all but disappeared. Cross-border travel now requires full immunology reports as an addendum to passport certifications. Such hassle is generally only undertaken by vacationers and those business travelers backed by large companies with fully staffed travel preparedness teams. In response, startups with automated solutions are popping up to help smaller enterprises fill the need for travel assistance.

While productivity is at a high thanks to digital connectivity, so is individual screen time. Attention spans and the ability to pull long hours are declining in both practice and desire. For the first time in history, the US sees a decrease in average weekly work hours. Citizens are embracing a new mindfulness around the division between work and life—spurred by a combination of digital exhaustion and a renewed search for tangible meaning. Simultaneously, average global weekly work hours have risen—rivaling those of the US for the first time. Opportunities for employment have shed their physical and geographic boundaries, engaging a truly global digital workforce and enabling cross-cultural shared practices.

Tangibly Local

While global digital connectivity is booming, global supply chains have never recovered. Grocers and food preparation services have transitioned into offering goods only to residents of their immediate surrounding neighborhoods as a form of community support through equitable distribution. Online orders now provide carrier provenance to aid shoppers in understanding where their orders have come from and with whom they have been.

Physical currency has disappeared from circulation as many businesses refuse to handle it, instead embracing a global cashless society. First popularized through platform services like Uber, Amazon, and Venmo, seamless transactions have integrated across the board. Big banks have reignited initiatives to open up payment APIs and embeddable services in order to comply with federal health and safety regulations.[32]

Coming out of the Great Isolation, younger generations led a cultural movement akin to the emergence of jazz in the Prohibition-era. Started through underground music, art, and social gatherings, these one-off events quickly evolved into small venues for niche engagement popping up in neighborhoods across the US. Foreclosed small businesses have converted their premises into late night gathering places for the creation of experiences that simultaneously represent the themes of isolation and serve as a break from it.

Individually Motivated

This social revival movement is in contrast to the trepidation many still feel when in crowds, leading to a confused work environment. For a vast majority, office buildings continue to feel exposed and unsafe, driving a reluctance to accept old ways of working. Businesses, looking to preserve their workforce, began by adopting a phased work schedule—allowing groups of employees back on-site during designated, rotating time slots.

Lasting effects from elongated periods of isolation, however, led to an increased rejection of over-regulation in the workplace. Combined with the complexity of scheduling, this quickly resulted in mass rejection of the rotation experiment. Given the evidence of productivity during the Great Isolation, many businesses are now opting for truly flexible remote work schedules.

A new digital modus operandi and desire to reduce workplace overheads spurred many businesses to decrease the amount of office space required—leaving many office buildings underutilized. City centers have been feeling this shift as urbanization slows and the work from home population spreads into surrounding suburbs and across state lines. With decreased business need and lower foot traffic, citizen groups have started reclaiming downtown streets.

A revived tactical urbanism movement is turning parking lots into art galleries, reintroducing native plants and trees, and creating pedestrian-first thoroughfares. City governments have recently begun engaging with these movements in an attempt to structure improvements collaboratively to align with local government goals and visions for urban center revitalization.

Overarching community engagement and global connectivity are emerging as early beneficial movements stemming from the pandemic of 2020. Federal governments, however, are just beginning to discuss how to turn efforts toward relief of racial, financial, and economic disparity felt prior to, and amplified by, the Great Isolation. If the last few years were a period of resocializing, the next few will be an era of restructuring.

- *What new post-pandemic planning practices would you like to see as urban cityscapes change and adapt to a new way of working?*
- *How do you think an increased focus on local supply chains could impact global relations?*
- *How do you think the adoption of virtual reality might impact business productivity?*

Alida Draudt is a foresight strategist, keynote speaker, and author of What the Foresight (Amazon, 2016). She lives and works in San Francisco, CA as a strategy director at AKQA and as an adjunct professor of Strategic Foresight in the DMBA program at California College of the Arts. alida.draudt@gmail.com

Navigating the Post-Pandemic Economy—Doing Business at the Speed of Change

By Robert Caldera

In the aftermath of the 2020 pandemic, how might companies change the way they work so that they are more resilient and responsive to sudden, disruptive events?

Long before the pandemic upended most businesses, organizations everywhere were under siege from the forces of relentless progress. Disruption has been exerting tremendous pressure on companies, in the form of digitization, the use of artificial intelligence (AI), globalization, shifting demographics, rapid urbanization, and climate change among other megatrends.

"The only constant in business is change," is a much-repeated phrase and, while true, the rate of change today has become exponential—creating even greater adaptation challenges. Things are likely to get increasingly difficult for the majority of today's companies that operate using a monolithic Industrial Age model. Most organizations simply don't have the wherewithal to thrive in an exponential world. It's as if they are using 18th-century armies to engage in modern warfare.

With few exceptions, in my experience, corporations evolve at a glacial pace. However, as with the planet's evolution, there are times when, spurred by external factors, sudden giant leaps forward occur. This global disease might just be the X-factor that spurs such a shift in the business world.

What might that leap look like over the next five years? Emergent thinking on the future of work backed by real examples of leading-edge organizations provide some clues. Below I set out one possible scenario of how these forces of change might come together in the near future, to reshape the way business is done in the world of 2025.

Remote Working

Remote work is now the norm rather than the exception. The experience of working from home throughout the pandemic shifted perspectives on work/life balance. The blurring of these lines created a greater appreciation for living lives not bound by artificial divisions of time and task. For some, the lack of those boundaries has been unwelcome, creating new forms of stress and anxiety for mental health professionals to tackle. In-person gatherings still occur, but that time is spent more wisely, largely in better, more collaborative experiences. This serves to strengthen bonds between staff who value the time together.

An era of greater trust between management and employees has emerged, driven by data showing that output and productivity actually increases when workers are operating remotely. But old habits die hard, and some companies push the boundaries of surveillance tool use to monitor employee activities using methods such as keystroke counts and webcam spying. In response, debates on privacy regulations have taken center stage in the political realm.

Distributed Organizations

The prevalence of remote workforces led to the rise of the distributed organization, as companies were forced to change the way they organize and work. Traditional top-down, command and control environments were already too slow for yesterday's business world. In a mostly virtual setting they became untenable.

Organizations shifted to network models that distribute work and responsibility in a way that allows for rapid decentralized decision-making. Some semblance of hierarchy remains as the old guard clutches to power, but inevitably self-management largely prevails. Autonomous teams, structured as microcosms of the entire company, are empowered to deliver the full value of what the company offers. Informal teams rapidly coalesce to meet specific needs before disbanding.

Contract Workforce

The percentage of independent contractors in the workforce—already a growing trend in 2020—has risen significantly, as distributed networks make it easy to rapidly plug holes with outsourced expertise. Some companies have made the dramatic shift to all contract workforces, with only a core group of employees left to truly champion the brand and culture. New legislation was passed aimed at safeguarding a contract workforce no longer protected by employer benefits. This is supported by tax code changes to reduce some of the financial burden of self-employment. Independence has led to more self-actualization and satisfaction with work.

Organizational Culture

Distributed networks have created conditions that motivate employees, such as autonomy and pursuit of mastery, but not all people are equipped to handle this. Individual responsibilities become clearer once removed from the blame chain of the corporate hierarchy. Unlike in a bureaucracy, you can't hide or just skate by. Plenty fall behind once exposed, especially older workers who struggle to adapt. Career-long learning has become a greater priority.

As a result, significant funds are put towards people development programs for employees and even contractors in some situations. Particular emphasis is placed on programs aimed at shifting mindsets, fostering adaptability, and building resilience. Those skilled in coaching, learning and development, and organizational psychology are in demand.

What constitutes culture has also been redefined in distributed organizations. Some companies lost their identity and morphed into something very different while others faded into obscurity. The rest have found creative ways to transition the "secret sauce" of their culture to this new structure. It is a time of considerable shuffling among the Fortune 500.

Enabling Technology

Technology, as expected, has played a substantial role in this changing business landscape. Decentralized organizations need decentralized platforms to help them succeed. Blockchain technology provides this, serving as the backbone of these organizations. Blockchain has improved transparency and data security while allowing individual contributions to become easily traceable. Much of the performance review and rewards process is now automated, minimizing bias.

Augmenting the ability to connect, collaborate, search, and share is paramount in this work environment. The Enterprise 2.0 revolution that never fully took off reignited with a wave of new AI-backed "Enterprise 3.0" tools. These next-generation social collaboration tools have become the thread that holds distributed organizations together.

Further, AI bots now aid employees in surfacing information, even before they realize they need it via predictive algorithms; bots automatically tag and store new information, take meeting minutes, and draft documents. It is the golden age of knowledge management. Every team has their own affable AI assistant.

Making Work More Human

In a post-pandemic world, redesigning organizations to keep pace with the rate of change becomes the new corporate obsession. Companies spend billions seeking ways to be more ready and responsive to disruptive events. Change readiness is achieved by companies that significantly enhance their communication, collaboration, and knowledge-sharing capabilities. These changes are enacted by workers for whom traits like adaptability, resiliency, and self-reliance have become second nature.

The shifts described in this chapter may have been a strong possibility even in a pre-pandemic world. However, they would have happened over a longer period through a slower process of change. The pandemic is a disruptor to this pattern and will likely accelerate us forward, bringing the future of work to the near present. This new way of working should enable greater opportunities for people to reach their full potential while creating more trusting, engaging, and relationship-driven cultures. How ironic that a pandemic preventing us from working together in-person could in the end be the catalyst for what makes work more human.

- *Will remote work become the norm rather than the exception in the post-pandemic business world?*
- *What might become of corporate culture in companies composed mostly of contingent workers who work remotely in distributed, autonomous teams?*
- *As AI becomes a necessary technology to enable the agility needed to thrive in a world where pandemics and other global-scale disruptive events occur more frequently, how far might businesses be willing to push the use of this technology?*

Rob Caldera is the owner of Future|Shift Consulting, a practice dedicated to helping clients anticipate and navigate disruptive change. Previously, Rob worked within the corporate world driving small- and large-scale change initiatives. He is certified in Strategic Foresight and as a Change Practitioner. rob@futureshiftconsulting.com

The Rise of Personal Digital Twins

By Roberto Saracco

How can we harness the exponential growth in life data to help individuals and society create actionable intelligence while protecting privacy?

In the end, the 2020 pandemic crisis turned out to be a strong driver in the reinvention of healthcare at a global level. Of course, it was a stressful period. The impact was significant from a personal and societal perspective, with so many people dying—particularly the elderly and health-compromised. The global economy was also hit hard, with the world's GDP declining by over US$5 trillion.

As we enter 2030, we need to look at the changes that have occurred in these last ten years; they have been so pervasive that we no longer notice them. Today, I have a digital replica of myself, called my personal digital twin.

Digital twins were widely used in industry even before 2020. Their use continually expanded in the last decade, pervading most sectors, from manufacturing to construction. They became a normal presence in retail and agriculture and supported the operation of cities and transportation. Twins are now indispensable at every level of every sector in the economy.

Digital transformation drove this growth by generating bits out of atoms and using those bits in design, manufacturing through 3D printers and robots, operations, and control. This evolution of "Industry 4.0" connected end users to the whole value chain and enabled progress towards the **"digitalization of the user"** to deliver a seamless stream of data from users' interactions with ever smarter, sensor laden products.

These personal digital twins were just an extension of user digital profiles that were already widely used in web services. Many apps had embedded features to monitor their use and the data were used to develop a model of user behavior. Of course, the big players like Amazon, Apple, Facebook, Google, Netflix, and others, evolved far more comprehensive and sophisticated user models since they had many more opportunities to observe user activity across their platforms. What started as profiling rapidly evolved into deeper contextualization of user behavior, enabling greater personalization and ever better assistance from intelligent assistants such as Alexa and Siri.

Indeed, the landscape of supporting technologies were coming into place ten years ago when the 2020 pandemic hit. In response, several countries scrambled to enforce the use of apps to monitor people and track the potential spread of contagion. Others were more indecisive, balancing the benefits of digital tracking and tracing against the risks to individual privacy.

However, as the pandemic affected more and more people the balance shifted towards greater adoption of such digital tools to help control the spread of the virus. This allowed unaffected people to continue working and socializing within a community and relieved pressure on the economy. The apps were a quick fix; it was natural to envision a more permanent framework that could be used beyond epidemic containment. They offered the ability to spot the first signs of an epidemic using personal, community, and society data. The more timely the availability of data, the more artificial intelligence (AI) could be used to predict its behavior, and the more data analytics could help pinpoint infection hotspots.

These developments propelled the adoption of personal digital twins. These were already being explored by companies like GE and Philips for applications in healthcare. Others, like IBM, the IEEE, and SAP, were looking at the use of personal digital twins in education and resource management.

Today, in 2030, personal digital twins are much more powerful than those first implementations. My digital twin receives continuous information on my physiology. The twin can monitor my heartbeat, breathing rhythms, temperature, glucose levels, and blood oxygenation from a few sensors I always carry with me. Some are embedded in my smartphone, watch, and other wearables, and in my home environment.

For example, every morning as I shave, the camera in the bathroom mirror picks up indicators from my facial, eye, and body movements. The data is transmitted to and analyzed by a personal healthcare app embedded in the operating system of my phone. Furthermore, my digital twin also maintains a permanent health record—storing information about my genome, the data from all of my medical examinations, and my prescriptions. More advanced digital twins can also store an individual's metabolome and proteome data.

All this data is continuously processed against the context of the environment I happen to be in. Hence, if I travel to another country, my twin seamlessly connects to the local healthcare framework and is immediately alerted to the presence of hotspots of infection. Conversely, if the analysis of my personal data points to a potential infection in my body, it releases this information to the healthcare system. Tracking and tracing has become instantaneous and ubiquitous.

My privacy is also being protected by my digital twin, which releases information on a need-to-know basis and only then to trusted parties, like the healthcare system. In case of contagion risk, I am immediately alerted with advice on safe behavior regardless of where I am. If I were to become infected, a personal care protocol will be established which might include enforcement of quarantine procedures and monitoring by the authorities. Of course, that means a temporary abdication of my privacy rights, but this is balanced by societal benefits that outweigh my personal freedoms.

All in all, I am better protected, and even more importantly, I feel safe. Of course, it is not just me; it is about most of us. The combination of post-pandemic concerns and the rise of digital twins has created a new culture. The expectation now is that healthcare is a societal effort and that as a society we should be proactive to avoid illness rather than scrambling to cure it; prevention is better than cure. Overall, healthcare costs have decreased, and the level of societal wellbeing has increased. This is not because of technology itself but because of the increased awareness provided by technology.

Not everyone has a personal digital twin, but there are a sufficient number of them to make epidemic detection and control highly effective. Importantly, attitudes towards personal digital twins have shifted from acceptance to desirability. In the coming years, they could well become a "must-have" and possibly a basic human right.

At this point, I no longer perceive my digital twin as a separate entity. We have become one and the same. It is augmenting me, and I cannot imagine a me without it.

- *Under what circumstances might we consider personal digital twins an integral part of ourselves?*
- *How should we balance privacy values against societal benefits in sharing personal health data?*
- *Given the growing volume of personal data, should it be used to help detect and contain potential epidemic hotspots?*

Roberto Saracco first worked in telecommunication networks and services research then shifted his interest to the economic and societal implications of technology. He led the Telecom Italia Future Centre in Italy and set up the Italian EIT Digital Node. He is a volunteer at IEEE and currently co-chairs the Digital Reality Initiative.
roberto.saracco@gmail.com

The Next Futures of Organizations, Work, and the Workplace

By Rohit Talwar, Steve Wells, and Alexandra Whittington

What new ways of organizational thinking and working could take hold or be abandoned as we move beyond the lockdown phase of the pandemic?

The pandemic crisis has been with us for just a short while and different countries are only months, weeks, or days into different degrees of lockdown or recovery. However, there has been a remarkably rapid impact on organizational activity and behavior, and we are already beginning to develop insights on the emerging possible futures of business, work, and the workplace. From a standing start, many entities have reshaped themselves to a model where the bulk of their workforce is operating from home.

For some, a total rethink of their strategy, business model, technology platforms, operating design, supply chain, and partnership ecosystem has been necessary. So, what's changing and how much of it could shape the next future of business, work, and the workplace? Here are ten shifts that organizations are having to embrace that could have lasting impacts.

1. The New Leadership

Leaders are beginning to appreciate the importance of flexibility and experimentation in everything from business models and distribution systems to the organization of work and the management of a largely home-based workforce. Empathy and emotionally literate leadership skills are becoming critical. The crisis is highlighting those who have the capacity to engage, motivate, and lead when all staff engagement is done via video and telephone. For example, in video mode, we may well be missing some of the subtle cues we might pick up in physical interactions.

Now, the best leaders are learning to acknowledge their own fears, uncertainties, and adaptation challenges, and to ask deeper questions that allow people to share their concerns and needs in a rapidly changing environment. Many roles are coming under greater scrutiny in a cost focused environment. For some in management and leadership roles the situation is quite exposing, as it reveals their jobs lacked substance or impact.

2. Innovation

Necessity is driving the generation of new possibilities at speed. Radical ideas are emerging or resurfacing for every challenge. At the macro level, previously unthinkable proposals are being considered and actioned, such as the notions of universal basic incomes (UBIs), compulsory health testing of an entire nation, total population lockdowns, and global flight bans. Organizationally, for many, innovation has become a true survival priority rather than just a budget line item.

The need for new ideas at speed is driving rapid experimentation and the results are often incredible. For example, massive global self-organizing networks have formed to share data, algorithms, and computing resources to tackle different aspects of modeling virus behavior. These collaborations are accelerating researchers' ability to generate, simulate, and test alternative medical solutions and response strategies. Similarly, prototypes for essential medical equipment have been designed and 3D printed in days rather than months or years.

The process of innovation is also being reimagined. Prior to the crisis, we had witnessed a continual growth in different facilitated innovation approaches. This is now being embraced in the virtual space. The need for variety in the online meeting experience is driving organizations to learn and trial a variety of approaches to generate and deliver innovations faster—from online task sprints to crowdsourcing.

3. Culture, Empowerment, and Trust

Major cultural challenges are emerging for predominantly office-based organizations where the physical environment helped shape and reinforce culture. They are learning to introduce virtual mechanisms to replace informal chats, the fly-by conversation, serendipitous water cooler encounters, and lunch and learn sessions. With most organizations still bedding down new ways of working and trying to react to market uncertainty and volatility, management is often highly preoccupied with the now, the near, and the next. Rapid waves of redundancies are also flattening some management structures and increasing spans of responsibility.

These changes and the speed at which events are unfolding have driven greater delegation of authority to enable individuals to respond to a rapidly changing reality. Allowing staff to take more responsibility, show more initiative, and make more decisions should also highlight the extent to which greater trust can be invested in the workforce going forward. The changes will also highlight where trust needs to be backed up by training, coaching, and review as people learn to operate with less supervision and instruction.

4. Prioritization and Decision-Making

The sheer scale of change and differing levels of impact are driving organizations to get smarter about project and task prioritization. Many are taking the opportunity to challenge the near- and medium-term value of every initiative and evaluate their chances of success under different post-pandemic scenarios. Focusing on the vital few is freeing up time and allowing the potential acceleration of new projects that respond to the changing opportunity landscape. In many cases, large digital transformation projects are being placed on hold. The emphasis and resources are shifting instead to truly transformational opportunities, for example using technologies such as artificial intelligence (AI), that could prove more fruitful in the new economy.

With meetings moving online, the willingness to learn and experiment with more participatory and collaborative decision-making approaches is growing. The simple act of a moderator controlling who can speak at any time in a group video chat changes the nature of discussion; people can finish their points without interruption, and everyone's voice can be heard. The loudest voices need not dominate. The crisis is also driving a willingness to experiment with crowdsourcing, collective intelligence, and group decision-making tools that offer a range of different and engaging ways of getting to decisions, appreciating differing perspectives, and reaching buy-in or consensus.

5. Learning

The situation is driving learning at every level which will provide organizations with a range of new capabilities and options. This starts from basic adaptation challenges such as how to work productively while your children are across the room doing homework or playing. The need to use remote working tools in particular is forcing people to acquire greater technology awareness. At a broader level, there is a strong imperative to raise our scientific literacy to understand concepts such as the basics of the disease, exponential growth, and the science behind social distancing.

At the macro level, leaders and employees alike are having to learn about notions like scenario thinking as they prepare for a wide range of possible futures. These range from scenarios for the evolution of the pandemic over the next few days, weeks, or months, through to the different possible economic outlooks for markets, nations, and the planet.

The removal of commuting time is also offering us the chance to learn new skills from mastering meditation and flower arranging to data science, AI, and behavioral economics—the take-up of online courses is on the rise. The benefits of a workforce that is constantly learning could become evident across many aspects of what organizations do in the future—from strategic thinking through to experimenting with new technologies and approaches.

6. Digital Literacy

By the end of the crisis we could well see a more digitally capable workforce. This could have massive benefits in terms of delivering technology change programs. Many are investing some commuting time savings to deepen their digital literacy—from learning productivity functions in Word and PowerPoint, to taking online classes in the technologies that could form part of their next task or job.

7. Productivity and Efficiency

Many are reporting that productivity and efficiency are improving through the reduction of workplace interruptions, cancellation of projects, and greater attention on clear communications. Individuals can focus more effectively on the task at hand, and learn the skills required to enhance their productivity. Research on telecommuting has consistently supported the idea that remote workers are more productive than their office-based counterparts. The pandemic may be a significant tipping point in the work-from-home trend if the majority of companies decide their employees should remain remotely based.

8. Flexibility and Adaptability

Organizationally, firms are developing new muscles—including the ability to adapt both what they do and how they do it—at speed. For example, around the world we see convention centers being repurposed as hospital restaurants catering for essential workers and takeaway delivery, and event organizers repositioning exhibitions and conferences as online offerings and community building activities. Others, such as grounded airlines, are having to face the challenge of laying off large numbers of flight crews or repurposing them to work on critical service innovations, and training that will help differentiate them when the recovery starts. Some are even supporting healthcare professionals in non-clinical roles in caring for infected patients.

Managers and workers are having to find workarounds for tasks they previously took for granted or never had to worry about. Organizations are constantly changing priorities, reshaping, cutting headcounts, and freezing hiring. In response, individuals are having to take on new roles, tasks, and responsibilities at speed and learn to develop rapport with others who they may not previously have encountered or managed. This is driving the demand for training in collaboration, cultural awareness, flexibility, adaptability, coping with chaos, and decision-making under uncertainty.

9. Collaboration and Ecosystems

New partnerships and collaborations are becoming commonplace—as evidenced by the unusual alliances forming between Formula One race teams and aviation equipment manufacturers to design and develop new ventilator solutions. How many other real-world challenges could these new ecosystems be harnessed to address?

Governments are working with the public, voluntary, and private sector to address challenges on a previously unseen and unimaginable scale. For example, over 750,000 people volunteered in days to support the UK National Health Service and wider society—in everything from transporting patients to delivering food to people in self-quarantine and calling on those in isolation.

Similarly, a range of resources and facilities have been mobilized to take all of the homeless off the streets within days—something that was previously considered a five- to ten-year challenge. Again, the question arises as to how many of these new solutions and ways of mobilizing resources at scale could become part of the fabric of civil society going forward.

10. Foresight, Scenario Thinking, and Resilience

For many, the crisis has highlighted the need to be better prepared for the unexpected as well as our "assumed or preferred future." This is driving demand for skills in horizon scanning for future risks and opportunities. From being a "nice to have," scenario planning is becoming a critical tool to explore different possible ways in which developments might combine and play out in the coming weeks, months, and years.

Some are also learning to use these future insights and scenarios to expand the range and severity of risk impacts factored into their resilience and recovery plans. For many, there is a growing recognition of the importance of having well thought through and properly tested contingency plans at national and organizational level. Of course, the supporting resources and mobilization protocols have to be in place to respond quickly, effectively, and assuredly. This can help avoid having to make too many decisions from scratch in the middle of an unfolding crisis.

The situation has presented organizations with a "not to be wasted" opportunity to acquire new approaches, ways of thinking, and skills that can help navigate the current crisis and lay the foundations for the next future of work.

- *How is the balance of conversation and focus shifting in your organization between addressing immediate operational challenges and thinking about future scenarios, strategies, and the organization of work?*
- *How are you and your organization managing the mental health risks associated with the lack of work-based social interaction through the switch to home working?*
- *What approaches—skills, tools, coaching support—are you and your organization deploying to maximize productivity?*
- *Which changes being implemented now to ensure operational continuity do you expect to remain in place post-pandemic?*

Conclusion—The Change Agenda for a Post-Pandemic World

By Rohit Talwar, Steve Wells, and Alexandra Whittington

What are the critical fragilities and opportunities that have to be part of the agenda recovery and future development at national and global level?

As the authors have demonstrated so vividly across the chapters of this book, there are many critical aspects to building a post-pandemic world; one that is fair, open, inclusive, sustainable, and rich in opportunities for all. The current crisis has surfaced a number of fragilities at the individual, societal, national, and international level. These have either been well understood but patchily addressed in the past, or are issues to which some or all are genuinely blindsided.

Fragilities also present the opportunity for genuinely new thinking and innovation. So, we conclude the book with what we consider to be ten key agenda items that we and the individual authors in this book believe will have to be part of the recovery agenda at national and global level.

1. Individual Financial Security and Sustainability

The crisis has highlighted that some people literally do not have enough savings to see them through the next month, week, or day. While for many, there was a vague acknowledgment of this as we went about our daily lives, it didn't truly seep into our consciousness or influence our behavior. Now, the massive expansion of people using foodbanks, coupled with the sight of mass population feeding programs in developing countries, has highlighted the scale of the problem and how far we have to go to resolve it—if that is seen as a priority.

Making real impact on the first two UN Sustainable Development Goals (SDGs) of "No Poverty" and "Zero Hunger" implies achieving a level of long-term individual sustainability. Governments will come under intense pressure to rethink social policy and to assess the suitability of welfare payments against broader questions of how long an individual or family can last with the money on offer. As a result, the debate about the need for some form of universal basic income (UBI) and services will inevitably rise in volume and intensity.

2. Health and Elder Care Systems and Access

The crisis has highlighted multiple issues around the level of provision, health and care worker salaries, resourcing levels, personal protective equipment (PPE), testing, logistics and distribution, managerial preparedness, resilience, and emergency planning. Every system globally will need to rethink its strategies, funding models, structures, early warning systems, and crisis protocols for a world where the awareness of the range of impending health risks has been heightened.

The poor state of people's finances has also left many with little or no ability to pay for care and limited access to emergency public provision. The funding of, and access to, healthcare for all could become an issue on which governments rise and fall.

3. Mental Health and Physical Safety

The number of cases of stress and other mental health conditions has seen a continuous rise in the last few years. The cost to society across multiple dimensions from healthcare to business interruption had already been estimated in the trillions of dollars. Now, during the pandemic, the loss of jobs, businesses, and freedoms amongst the old and young alike are reported to be driving up the volume and severity of stress and other mental health issues across society. For governments, there will be issues around the extent to which they want to intervene, ensuring access, the capacity to serve growing demand, and the funding of such services.

A related issue is that globally, there has been a clear, and in some cases massive, rise in reported cases of domestic abuse, calls to helplines, and the unseen suffering of those not in a position to ask for help. Once the recovery starts, non-interventionist governments in particular are going to be challenged to determine the priority placed on such matters. The resulting choices will have far-reaching implications for funding of support services from social services and policing through to healthcare and education.

4. National Preparedness

The crisis has put a spotlight on the huge differences in the level of preparedness and capacity for rapid action in different nations around the world. Some had well tested procedures to mobilize travel restrictions, and enact mass testing, tracing, and quarantine measures. They also had systems and policy options in place to be able to carry out a diverse range of support measures. These range from calling up reservist health workers and making direct payments to the population, through to mobilizing volunteers and communities at scale. Others seemed, and still appear to be, incapable or leaden footed in their actions. This will raise the debate about the need for national mechanisms for horizon scanning and foresight, risk assessment, anticipatory contingency and disaster planning, and resilient resourcing to enable rapid scale-up in emergencies.

5. Funding

Most nations have looked to debt, quantitative easing, and the printing of money to fund their way through the emergency medical and economic response programs they have had to implement. The question is how, or if, these bills will be paid. The general trend over the last two decades or more has been to drive down taxes in the hope that greater wealth in the economy will raise everyone's living standards. The crisis has highlighted that this isn't really working anywhere near as well as policy makers might have hoped in many countries across the globe.

The crisis has been expensive, the cost of recovery is as yet unknown as we face the prospect of prolonged national recessions or even a global depression. Nations may be forced to reverse taxation policy as they look to corporations, higher earners, and the wealthy to provide more of the funding to restart economies currently stuck in reverse gear. The alternative could be massive cuts in public services and government spending, resulting in prolonged periods of austerity—with all the social consequences such measures bring.

The specter of mass technological unemployment was already on the horizon due to the rise of automation technologies and artificial intelligence (AI) in particular. This in turn had driven the debate over the potential for introducing a UBI—and how it might be funded—with options ranging from taxes on wealth, financial transactions, or the deployment of AI and robotics. These mechanisms are now back in the spotlight as countries wrestle with how to pay the bill for the pandemic and finance the economic and social recovery.

6. Government and Governance

The challenge for every government is to find the right future governance, engagement, and representation models for populations that have probably never placed the actions of their political leaders under such close examination. National governments have come under intense scrutiny during the pandemic. The spotlight has been placed on their level of foresight, disaster preparedness, and capacity to make crucial decisions in the middle of a crisis. Equally questions are being asked about how well the lessons are being learned both for the next stage of the crisis and for the future. Issues of transparency, honesty, planning assumptions, and priorities are all coming to the fore as populations ask whether their governments are doing a good job.

At the same time, governments are using a variety of community mechanisms and technology tools to innovate solutions to the myriad of issues and needs that arise. Decisions about the use of emergency powers and citizen surveillance tracking and tracing tools are raising questions about the future protection of civil liberties and privacy. Stay at home orders have driven many civil servants to work from home. Hence, questions are also being raised about how effectively the work of governments can be delivered from our dining tables while home schooling our children.

7. Global Institutions

The World Health Organization has come under severe criticism from some quarters and been seen by others as an essential resource and partner in navigating the crisis. The United Nations and global financial institutions such as the World Bank have been visible, but the question is how impactful they have been. The remit and rules of engagement for these institutions are set by their member and donor states. The key questions now are whether those rules are the right ones and whether these global organizations are truly fit for purpose when it comes to global crisis where coordinated solutions are required. If the answer is at least a partial no, then how do we go about modernizing or replacing them, who will fund them, and how can we ensure greater effectiveness than the existing entities they are replacing?

8. Weak and Failing Nations

There is growing concern that the crisis will cause chaos in nations already on the brink of collapse such as Afghanistan, Syria, and Yemen. Some estimates suggest that these and other under-resourced and overstretched nations could see three million or more deaths from the pandemic. The question is how such nations can map a path to the future. Do they effectively seek protection from other states, merge into larger entities, or become the testbed for radical new models of post-conflict, post-crisis government and governance?

9. Coordination of Global Power

Many would argue that in the Global Financial Crisis of 2007-2008, the worst-case scenario of total economic collapse was avoided through the coordinated efforts of the wealthiest nations in the G7 and G20 groupings. However, this time round, they have been noticeable by their absence and their inability to even issue joint communiques over how they are coming together to tackle what is a truly global problem. Without the wealth, resources, and mobilization capabilities of these nations acting together, the crisis could stretch out far longer than the 12- to 24-month window that many are predicting.

10. The Business of Business and the Environment

The crisis has raised a number of interesting questions over the future role and purpose of business and how we truly balance the quadruple bottom line of people, planet, purpose, and prosperity. The UN Sustainable Development Goals (SDGs) have become an increasingly important filter through which businesses run their strategies, and that focus is likely to increase. Some argue that this is the beginning of the end of capitalism in its current form and that new models need to be tested that result in a fairer distribution of wealth and resources.

The slowdown of economic activity has had a powerful impact on the environment with marked declines in emissions and air pollution. Natural habitats have blossomed, and rarely spotted animal species have become more visible. The planet has been given the chance to rest and recuperate from the frenetic pace of human activity. The issues now are whether those gains can be sustained as economic activity ramps up and what priority governments and businesses place on the environment as they seek to recover from the financial impacts of the pandemic.

The advent of exponential technologies such as AI and synthetic biology offer the potential for deep and dramatic transformation of every sector and the unleashing of economic abundance. The question arises as to how the spoils will be divided and what happens to those whose roles are replaced by the technology. If new jobs are to be created for these new sectors, then who will bear the cost of retraining the workforce?

Governments are providing and promising a wide range of financial support measures to help businesses through the crisis. There is a question over the extent to which these rescue packages are being tied to environmental, social, innovation, and job creation goals. Ultimately, the question will need to be asked as to what businesses think their role is in tomorrow's world and what responsibilities they bear to the environment and wider society?

The crisis is raising fundamental questions at every level and creating once in a lifetime challenges for those in power. Many are still wrestling with the complexities of containment and exit strategies and have little bandwidth for broader medium- to long-term considerations. Others are beginning to understand that the crisis represents both a turning point and a time for fundamental reflection. What are the goals for human life, society, nations, and the globe that we want to enable on the other side of the pandemic? Fortunately, we have the SDGs as a start point for that reflection—the question will be how big our appetite is to use this opportunity to drive fundamental changes in our destiny.

- *What should governments prioritize as they lay out the change agenda for the next one, five, and ten years?*
- *Do societal health, mental wellbeing, and physical security have to take a back seat as governments focus on restarting the economic engine?*
- *How can we ensure that delivering on the Sustainable Development Goals becomes even more central to the delivery of national recovery plans and corporate strategies for the near to medium term?*

References

1. Yergin, D. 2009. 'A crisis in search of a narrative'. *Financial Times*, 20 October 2009. *https://www.ft.com/content/8a82d274-bda9-11de-9f6a-00144feab49a*

2. Roy, A. 2020. 'The pandemic is a portal'. *Financial Times*, 3 April 2020. *https://www.ft.com/content/10d8f5e8-74eb-11ea-95fe-fcd274e920ca*. Accessed 7 April 2020

3. Personal email. 6 April 2020.

4. *https://i.redd.it/0c1rr8w779n41.png*. Accessed 6 April 2020.

5. Sarkar, P.R. 1987. *Prout in a Nutshell*. Kolkata: Prout Publications.

6. Jones, C. 1997. 'Cosmic Gaia' in Galtung, J and Inayatullah, *S. Macrohistory and Macrohistorians*. Westport: Ct. Praeger.

7. Inayatullah, S. 2017. *Prout in Power: Policy Solutions that Reframe our Futures*. Delhi: Prout Publications.

8. RNA (ribonucleic acid) and DNA (deoxyribonucleic acid) are chemicals called nucleotides that are made by the body (Web MD).

9. Musu, C. 2020. 'War metaphors used for COVID-19 are compelling but also dangerous'. *The Conversation*, 19 March 2020. *https://theconversation.com/war-metaphors-used-for-covid-19-are-compelling-but-also-dangerous-135406*

10. Little, W. 2014. *Introduction to Sociology - *1st Canadian Edition. BCcampus. Chapter 7 – Deviance, Crime and Social Control. *https://opentextbc.ca/introductiontosociology/chapter/chapter7-deviance-crime-and-social-control/*

11. Pose, F. 2020. 'Social distancing? Working-class people don't have that luxury'. *The Guardian*, 1 April 2020. *https://www.theguardian.com/commentisfree/2020/apr/01/coronavirus-covid-19-working-class*

12. Russel, A. 2020. 'The rise of coronavirus hate crimes'. *The New Yorker*, 17 March 2020. *https://www.newyorker.com/news/letter-from-the-uk/the-rise-of-coronavirus-hate-crimes*

13. Perrigo, B. 2020. 'White Supremacist Groups Are Recruiting With Help From Coronavirus – and a Popular Messaging App'. *Time*, 8 April 2020. *https://time.com/5817665/coronavirus-conspiracy-theories-white-supremacist-groups/*

14. De Poloni, G. 2020. 'How coronavirus could forever change the look and feel of Australia's cities and suburbs'. *The Age*, 10 April 2020. *https://www.abc.net.au/news/2020-04-11/how-coronavirus-could-forever-change-our-cities-and-suburbs/12137122*

15. OECD. 2014. 'Is migration good for the economy?'. *Migration Policy Debates*, May 2014. *https://www.oecd.org/migration/OECD%20Migration%20Policy%20Debates%20Numero%202.pdf*

16. Coates, B., et al. 2020. *Shutdown: estimating the COVID-19 employment shock.* Grattan Institute. *https://grattan.edu.au/wp-content/uploads/2020/04/Shutdown-estimating-the-COVID-19-employment-shock-Grattan-Institute.pdf*

17. Arakkal, S. 2020. 'Millennials are driven to a hard generational bargain'. *The Sydney Morning Herald*, 6 April 2020. *https://www.smh.com.au/national/millennials-are-driven-to-a-hard-generational-bargain-20200402-p54ga1.html*

18. Grattan Institute. 2020. *Webinar: The economic, budgetary and health impacts of Covid-19. https://grattan.edu.au/events/the-economic-budgetary-and-health-impacts-of-covid-19-webinar/*

19. Europol. 2020. *Pandemic Profiteering: how criminals exploit the COVID-19 crisis. https://www.europol.europa.eu/publications-documents/pandemic-profiteering-how-criminals-exploit-covid-19-crisis*

20. Harari, Y. N. 2020. 'Yuval Noah Harari: the world after coronavirus'. *Financial Times*, 20 March 2020. *https://www.ft.com/content/19d90308-6858-11ea-a3c9-1fe6fedcca75*

21. Future Agenda. 2020. *Proof of Immunity and the Demise of Privacy. https://www.futureagenda.org/foresights/proof_of_immunity/*

22. Bell, G. 2020. 'We need mass surveillance to fight Covid-19 – but it doesn't have to be creepy'. *MIT Technology Review*, 12 April 2020. *https://www.technologyreview.com/2020/04/12/999186/covid-19-contact-tracing-surveillance-data-privacy-anonymity/*

23. Goudarzi, S. 2020. 'How a Warming Climate Could Affect the Spread of Diseases Similar to COVID-19'. *Scientific American*, 29 April 2020. *https://www.scientificamerican.com/article/how-a-warming-climate-could-affect-the-spread-of-diseases-similar-to-covid-19/*

24. DePaulo, B. 2020. 'What We Need Now: 3 Types of Cocooning'. *Psychology Today*, 7 March 2020. *https://www.psychologytoday.com/us/blog/living-single/202003/what-we-need-now-3-types-cocooning*

25. Stewart, H. 2009. 'This is how we let the credit crunch happen, Ma'am'. *The Guardian*, 26 July 2009. *https://www.theguardian.com/uk/2009/jul/26/monarchy-credit-crunch*

26. Nuki, P. 2020. 'Exercise Cygnus uncovered: the pandemic warnings buried by the government'. *The Telegraph*, 28 March 2020. *https://www.telegraph.co.uk/news/2020/03/28/exercise-cygnus-uncovered-pandemic-warnings-buried-government/*

27. Gates, B. 2015. *The next outbreak: We're not ready. TED. https://www.ted.com/talks/bill_gates_the_next_outbreak_we_re_not_ready*

28. London Futurists. 2020. *Risks beyond Covid-19*. YouTube. *https://www.youtube.com/watch?v=ce02pCOre0U*

29. Lanier, J and Weyl, E.G. 2020. 'How Civic Technology Can Help Stop a Pandemic'. *Foreign Affairs*, 20 March 2020. *https://www.foreignaffairs.com/articles/asia/2020-03-20/how-civic-technology-can-help-stop-pandemic*

30. Berditchevskaia, A. and Peach, K. 2020. *Coronavirus: seven ways collective intelligence is tackling the pandemic.* World Economic Forum, 15 March 2020. *https://www.weforum.org/agenda/2020/03/coronavirus-seven-ways-collective-intelligence-is-tackling-the-pandemic/*

31. Bloom, N., Liang, J., Roberts, J. and Ying, Z.J. 2015. 'Does working from home work? Evidence from a Chinese experiment', *Quarterly Journal of Economics*, 165-218. doi:10.1093/qje/qju032. *https://nbloom.people.stanford.edu/sites/g/files/sbiybj4746/f/wfh.pdf*

32. API stands for Application Programming Interface which allows different types of software to interact.

Also from Fast Future

THE AIR TRANSPORT 2035 REPORT SERIES
Working in partnership with Future Travel Experience, we have developed a series of reports exploring key aspects of the near- and long-term future of the Air Transport Sector in the post-pandemic era. The four reports are:

COVID-19 Air Transport Near-Term Impacts and Scenarios
This report presents the results of an industry survey, expert interviews, desk research and analysis to explore the impacts of the pandemic on the sector and present scenarios for the possible near-term evolution of the sector. The detailed results cover the immediate and full year impact on flights/passenger numbers/revenues, expectations for the timing of peak impact, recovery timescales, redundancies, people and skills development priorities, finance and operations strategies, longer-term operating assumptions and tactics, longer-term financial and ownership assumptions and tactics, investment priorities, procurement implications, critical response priorities/strategies/tactics, implications for longer-term sector strategy, and key learnings from the sector's response to the pandemic to date.

The Impacts of COVID-19 on Innovation and Digital Transformation in Air Transport
This report highlights the results of an industry survey, expert interviews, desk research and analysis to explore how the pandemic is shaping approaches to innovation and digital transformation across

the sector. The detailed results cover the response to COVID-19 in terms of changes to the terminal environment, technology use in the airport environment, impact on cabin configuration and in-flight experience, longer-term airport and airline innovation priorities and developments, impact on digital transformation and collaboration strategies, and implications for innovation and digital transformation budgets and longer-term strategies.

Air Transport 2035
–Long-Term Drivers, Opportunities, and Challenges –
Available September 2020

This report is timed to coincide with the point where most expect that travel bans will be lifting, and the sector will be making detailed plans for how to navigate the next few years. The report will draw on a global industry survey, expert interviews, wide-ranging research, and detailed analysis. It will highlight the drivers that could shape the longer-term future of the sector and emphasize the critical importance of ensuring present-day thinking takes account of the longer-term possibilities, opportunities, and challenges.

The aim is to ensure that crisis driven decisions don't close the door to future options. Key topics covered will include external drivers of change, long-term implications of the current pandemic, airport infrastructure and terminal design, airport technology and the passenger experience, the in-flight travel experience and service developments, airport and airline commercial strategies and business models, aircraft technology developments, the future use of information and technology and artificial intelligence in aviation, passenger use of technology, and environmental strategies.

Air Transport 2035
–Long-Term Scenarios, Strategies, and Roadmaps –
Available December 2020

This report will pull together the findings of the three previous studies and our wide-ranging program of research. It will set out detailed scenarios for how the sector and key parts of the air transport ecosystem could play out over the longer term. It will go on to highlight a range of strategies and roadmaps for the possible evolution of different organizations of varying size across the sector.

OPPORTUNITY AT THE EDGE
–Change, Challenge, and Transformation on the Path to 2025

Opportunity at the Edge, developed by Fast Future in collaboration with Aruba, reports that edge technologies—those which process and analyze user data where people connect to a network—will revolutionize corporate strategies, create more dynamic, responsive, and personalized customer and employee experiences, enable powerful business and revenue models, and even catalyze the growth of entirely new industries. To unlock these opportunities, the book argues that enterprises must embrace fundamental change, engaging in widespread strategic, structural, and leadership transformation.

Morten Illum, VP EMEA at Aruba, comments: "The findings in this book highlight the vast commercial potential for enterprises utilizing edge technologies, if companies are willing and able to enact the considerable organizational changes needed. The edge represents a dramatic overhaul in how companies understand, service, and meet the needs of their customers and employees. It will be a world defined by dynamic, immediate, and personalized services."

A VERY HUMAN FUTURE
–Enriching Humanity in a Digitized World

As society enters the fourth industrial revolution, a major question arises—can we harness intense technological bursts of possibility to bring about a better world? *A Very Human Future* illustrates how the evolution of society, cities, people, businesses, industries, nations, and governments are being unexpectedly entangled by exponential technological disruption. This is not a book about technology but an exploration of how we make it serve humanity's highest needs and ambitions. Each chapter looks at how new ideas enabled by emerging technologies are straining the old social fabric, and proposes radical future scenarios, strategies, and actions to safeguard humanity from harm and enhance opportunity for all. This book is a manifesto for a future that is better than the past.

A Very Human Future rejects an outlook where human beings live a mundane existence while technologies burst with possibility. Rather, we use this book to endorse a proactive approach to the future where technology is designed to benefit humanity purposefully and intentionally. To advocate for a very human future we ask, for example, how do we use technology to overcome gender bias or to impart a meaningful education to new generations? Can artificial intelligence tools make government more trustworthy and help us deal with the impacts of automation replacing humans? What rights should people have when residing in smart cities? The scale of the new technologies requires a protective logic for moving forward, keeping humanity at the center so that we avoid dehumanizing ourselves and future generations.

A Very Human Future is not one, but many positive stories and visions of the future that can be powerful beacons for social adaptation. We argue that the time to control the narrative of the future and stake a claim for humanity is now. *A Very Human Future* uses knowledge as power, describing surprising ways new thinking and disruptive technology can impact society. This book explains that protecting what's human is the key to retaining our dominance over future technological progress.

BEYOND GENUINE STUPIDITY
–Ensuring AI Serves Humanity

The first book in the *Fast Future* series explores critical emerging issues arising from the rapid pace of development in artificial intelligence (AI). The authors argue for a forward-looking and conscious approach to the development and deployment of AI to ensure that it genuinely serves humanity's best interest. Through a series of articles, they present a compelling case to get beyond the genuine stupidity of narrow, short-term, and alarmist thinking and look at AI from a long-term holistic perspective. The reality is that AI will impact current sectors and jobs—and hopefully enable new ones.

A smart approach requires us to think about and experiment with strategies for adopting and absorbing the impacts of AI—encompassing education systems, reskilling the workforce, unemployment and guaranteed basic incomes, robot taxes, job creation, encouraging new ventures, research and development to enable tomorrow's industries, and dealing with the mental health impacts. The book explores the potential impacts on sectors ranging from healthcare and automotive, to legal and education. The implications for business itself are also examined from leadership and HR, to sales and business ethics.

THE FUTURE REINVENTED
–Reimagining Life, Society, and Business

The second book in the *Fast Future* series explores the future transformations that could arise from the disruptive technological, scientific, social, and economic developments shaping the decade ahead. The authors offer a range of unique visions of different aspects of a future in which the very tenets of reality are undergoing deep and vital transformations. Through a series of chapters organized into three sections (transformations in life, industries, and business), they present holistic future scenarios that encourage strategic thinking about what lies beyond the hype.

Using a long-term futurist perspective, *The Future Reinvented* offers glimpses of the future in different business sectors such as legal, automotive, and sales as well as in different areas of everyday life like retirement, education, and health. Audiences will appreciate the vivid imagery which brings to life a number of different "futures," including workplace scenarios where people work side by side with artificial intelligence or robotic colleagues, can obtain physical enhancements to become smarter, stronger, or more psychologically resilient, or reside in a post-jobs world. The book provides a solid foundation for scenario thinking and planning, identifying signals of change, and interpreting signposts that serve as early warning signs for emerging futures.

THE FUTURE OF BUSINESS
–Critical insights to a rapidly changing world from 62 future thinkers

The Future of Business is aimed at the leaders of today and the pioneers of tomorrow. Our intention is to provide a broad perspective on the key forces, trends, developments, and ideas that could redefine our world over the next two decades. The goal is to highlight how these future factors are shaping the opportunities, challenges, implications, and resulting choices for those driving the future of business. The book draws on the ideas of 62 futurists, future thinkers, and experts in a range of domains from 22 countries on four continents. *The Future of Business* highlights how—in a world of constant and ever-more fundamental change—those charged with leadership, management, and stewardship of large and small organizations alike are faced with a set of questions many of us never thought we would have to confront. This book is designed to provide wide-ranging visions of future possibilities and take us on a tour of the forces shaping the political, economic, and social environment. We explore the advances in science and technology that could have the greatest impact on society and drive business disruption. We examine the implications of these for how business will need to evolve and the new industries that could emerge over the next two decades. We highlight key tools, approaches, and ways of thinking about the future that can help organizations embed foresight at the heart of the management model. We conclude with a framework that highlights key choices we face in shaping *The Future of Business.*

Available soon from Fast Future

50:50—Scenarios for the Next 50 Years

This book explores scenarios for the next 50 years, with 50 perspectives on possible futures from 50 different future thinkers around the world. The book is designed to have the broadest possible scope and is edited by global futurists Rohit Talwar, Steve Wells, and Alexandra Whittington. The book explores potential future scenarios over the next 50 years across a range of topic areas.

Future Publications

The landscape for potential publication topics is evolving rapidly and we are excited at the prospects of working on multi-author books or partnering with innovative organizations who share our passion for exploring the future. We are currently considering books on a range of future related themes.

We are always interested to hear from authors who want to bring their ideas, knowledge, and insights to market with Fast Future.

Visit *www.fastfuture.com* for more information.

Introduction
—The Future Reinvented

The Future Reinvented –
Reimagining Life, Society, and Business

The Future Reinvented – Reimagining Life, Society, and Business is an invitation to explore alternative—and sometimes competing—perspectives on how our collective futures may play out. The challenge for all of us is to try and form plausible but sufficiently stretching views of how the next decade could unfold under the influence of an ever-growing array of often exponentially accelerating forces of change.

Humanity today really does sit in the eye of a fast-moving storm that is combining and reinforcing major drivers of change from across the spectrum. These encompass politics, macro-economics, business and commerce, society, demographics, science, technology, energy, the environment, laws and regulations, moral choices, and our ethical frameworks.

When we take a step back to examine this constantly evolving and emerging landscape, it becomes clear that most of us have been, and perhaps still are, basing our planning assumptions on an expected future that is unlikely to materialize. On the contrary, these forces are breaking with tradition and expectation and are developing in unpredictable ways and at a pace few of us can keep up with. In short, we are witnessing a total transformation of the expected future, encompassing every aspect of life on our planet. This is the story we are exploring in *The Future Reinvented – Reimagining Life, Society, and Business*.

This second book in the **Fast Future** series, explores the major trends, forces, developments, and ideas shaping the next future. Our aim is to highlight how society's received wisdom, assumptions, and collective notions of the future are themselves undergoing a process of reinvention. Our goal is to encourage readers to challenge both "the official view" and your own perspectives on which changes will have the most impact. Our intention is to help you reimagine how life, society, key industries, and the conduct of business could be transformed in the decade ahead.

The Past is Not a Roadmap or a Destination

Often when organizations and individuals try to envision their future, they base their visions and strategies on solving past and current challenges. They try to project current trends into the future, and naturally assume or hope that progress will happen at a relatively steady, evolutionary pace. Technology inevitably plays a starring role in any such future narrative, even if we are a little sketchy on the implementation detail.

Interestingly, those that do have a sense of how deeply exponential technologies could impact our world can be somewhat overawed by the scale of potential changes and the societal implications. Those who seek answers or reassurance tend to be left unsatisfied with the responses to their concerns; indeed, in the name of progress, governments, the technology community, and techno-progressive thinkers often swat aside questions over whether the technology can actually deliver the goods, how society might react, and how we ensure fair and open access to such life-governing advances. In fact, they use past industrial revolutions and technological disruptions as evidence that human ingenuity has always left humanity better off.

The core arguments of the techno-optimists are that firstly the concerns being raised over issues like technological unemployment don't take account of the opportunities that will be created in sectors and businesses that don't yet exist. Secondly, they suggest that these technologies will deliver abundance and hence eliminate the need for us to work in dangerous or tedious jobs. They envisage a miraculous shift in public consciousness, where being unemployed is seen as a way of being that allows us to pursue our true purpose and express ourselves as oil painters, poets, and landscape gardeners.

Clearly, exponential technologies will undoubtedly play a fundamental part of our daily lives. In some quarters, there is almost breathless excitement at the increasing blurring of boundaries between the realms of science fantasy or magic and the technological realities that are unfolding. In every aspect of life, society, and business there are a seemingly endless array of opportunities emerging today or on the not too distant horizon.

However, perhaps our biggest challenge and opportunity is ensuring humanity survives and thrives in this technological utopia. We cannot place blind faith in technology to solve our biggest global challenges. Nor can we assume that artificial intelligence (AI) will always make choices that maximize the benefit to the largest number of people. We are at point in history where a wake-up call is resonating across the planet. In this book, we aim to highlight how we can heed that call and harness the immense power of science and technology to help us reimagine life, society, and business in a manner that ensures a very human future for all.

Embracing the Fourth Industrial Revolution

Historically, each economic revolution has been characterized by the introduction of science and technology breakthroughs that accelerated the production and distribution of goods and services. The First Industrial Revolution between 1760 and 1840 gave birth to the iron and textile industries and saw the use of water and the steam engine to mechanize production and power new factories across Europe and America. The transition from agrarian to industrial economy saw a reduction of physical labor demand in rural areas. Job opportunities shifted to the cities, and people followed the money to ensure their survival.

The Second Industrial Revolution took place between 1870 and 1914, and heralded advances such as electricity, the light bulb, and the telephone, which in turn enabled rapid industrialization and globalization. Established industrial sectors were disrupted, new ones emerged, and key infrastructure services were expanded rapidly, including rail networks, and public gas, water, and sewage systems. Production lines, nightshifts, and lower transportation costs changed social dynamics within families, communities, and workplaces.

The Third Industrial Revolution, or "Digital Revolution," started around 1969 with the rise of nuclear power, a shift to microelectronics from analog and mechanical devices, and the resulting development of sectors such as space exploration and biotechnology. Globalization contributed to this next wave of change—and was accelerated by it—pushing people together and accelerating the development of cities.

The convergence of information and communication technologies (ICT) and the rise of the Internet are perhaps the main symbols of the global impact of this revolution. The transformation from analog to digital revealed that software is cheaper and more efficient than salaried employees, which in turn pushed workers from manufacturing to the service industries. Unfortunately, better technology has not necessarily guaranteed enough or better jobs for all.

According to the World Economic Forum, we are entering an era of smart technologies, and a Fourth Industrial Revolution is emerging which will see us incorporate these advances into societies and humans themselves.[1] Following Moore's law, technology that was available a decade ago is becoming better. Most fields of ICT are progressing at least exponentially, enabling more functions, and are easily accessible through a plethora of applications and devices.

We've entered an era where general-purpose technologies like computers, tablets, and smartphones can perform a myriad of tasks just by changing the software. This set of mainly mobile hardware platforms provides the foundation for the waves of digital transformation now sweeping the planet and encompassing every aspect of human activity.

The exponentially progressing science and technology developments shaping the Fourth Industrial Revolution include: augmented reality (AR), artificial intelligence, autonomous vehicles, big data, biomimicry, blockchain, cloud computing, DNA computing, drones, genetics, human brain and body enhancements, hyperconnectivity, the

Internet of things (IoT), nanotechnology, smart materials, organic and synthetic chemistry, quantum computing, renewable energy, robotics, sensors, synthetic biology, virtual reality (VR), and 3D/4D printing.

The key here is that the seeds of the next future are already planted and growing fast. Whether applied individually or in combination with each other, this array of innovations could dramatically impact life, society, and business in the near future. Across the globe, people are developing, researching, regulating, and consuming the early stages of these advancements. The choices these individuals make every day serve to nudge the future in a certain direction—but they are not all heading the same way, which makes the uncertainty of the outcomes even more interesting.

Decision making is largely based on historic data, in the form of experience or knowledge, which anticipates an outcome. Social values and cultural practices also influence this process by providing general moral guidelines. However, the future will not necessarily resemble the past and these technologies are already altering our moral compasses. Individuals' behavior, relationships, and expectations are shifting because of technology, but this cause-and-effect relationship is reciprocal. So, how can we help others prepare for the impacts the Fourth Industrial Revolution might have on their lives, society, and businesses?

Exploring the Next Future

The Future Reinvented – Reimagining Life, Society, and Business is designed to help expand our current decision-making process by considering alternative visions of the future and challenging our biases, as individuals and organizations. Each chapter explores a different aspect of the possible future and raises questions to help us think about the ways in which the developments being discussed could have an impact for individuals, societies, businesses, and governments.

Whilst we have included some more playful and exploratory predictions, the majority of the chapters focus on exploring a range of possible scenarios and conditional "what if" questions. These are powerful tools for exploring different possible outcomes when a range of forces come together. As futurists, we are trained to ask our clients and ourselves these questions on a constant basis. The reasoning behind this is that the future is not a defined destination, but on the contrary, a set of chaotic paths where the slightest change in the starting conditions or direction of travel could influence the end outcome quite dramatically. Thus, instead of trying to predict and plan for the prime or preferred scenario, the futurist approach is to try and create a comprehensive and resilient strategy that takes into consideration a range of different possible futures.

However, in order to reinvent the future, we need to unveil and understand what our current driving assumptions and default images are of how the next decade may play out. Only by assessing where we are starting from can we begin to think about different possibilities to the "almost probable certain future" we had been planning for and how to get somewhere else. This part of the process is about challenging our own biases.

Although our preconceived notions may seem harmless or unrelated to planning for the future, they may be blocking our ability to grasp opportunities or challenges on the horizon. We may be clinging on to ideas about how the world and our markets operate that are no longer a valid or helpful abstraction, or a good working simplification, of how things work. In fact, they may be taking us down a potentially dangerous alley that could lead to bad life choices or the failure of our organization.

Opening up to new ideas, different perspectives, and totally different ways of thinking about the future in general, and in our sector in particular, is critical to the process of conceiving alternative possible futures. We can explore diverse perspectives on the future by talking to those already embracing a different worldview, and metaphorically stepping into the shoes of competitors and new entrants who are pursuing wildly divergent strategies to ourselves. We can also tap into different futures perspectives both by consulting players across our value chain and by working with diverse teams within the business to help develop insight into, and empathy for, their views on how the world is changing.

The last part of reinventing our path to future is understanding how time sensitive the actions are. A small variation in the pace of change could lead to a very different set of futures: Being second or third to market with a new proposition might help us save on market development costs, but would still allow us to take advantage of scarcity, novelty, and premium pricing opportunities; being among the last to enter may mean we are already competing in a low margin, commoditized space before we've gained any learning to drive efficiencies in the cost of our go-to market offerings and delivery processes.

In a complex world where wicked problems are comprised of many different, interconnected, and fast changing parts, timing is everything. A small delay can lead to yet another related issue coming onto our radar, or more competitors entering the market and redefining expectations around the characteristics and pricing of the offering. Hence, this book highlights examples of ideas, issues, forces, trends, and developments that we should be discussing and acting on in the near future before they shift from being enticing opportunities, to challenges, or crises.

Reframing Life

Reimagining life implies forming new creative and resourceful ideas, images, and concepts of how we might live in the future; conceiving how we might harness technology innovations to service humanity's best interests. As mentioned above, in the past, the introduction of revolutionary technologies has impacted humanity at different levels. Moving to the city, using electricity, teleworking, and sharing across the Internet have all been life changing events enabled by technological advances. Now these activities have become part of normal life.

So, how quickly would we take it for granted if our next vehicle could drive itself or fly? Where would you go? How would you use it? How would that change where you live or the relationship you have with your family? Moreover, would you buy it, lease it, or just subscribe to its services? How would this influence the way you perceive its primary purpose, your definition of a car, and what you do in it? Similar types of questions apply to every technology that could impact our world. For example, what if our smartphone in 2020 could run our daily lives and conduct conversations on our behalf?

Imagine this avalanche of questions and uncertainties that will arise when it's not only your automobile that is smarter. What happens when there is intelligence built into the appliances in your home, the software at work, the gadgets and toys used by kids to learn and play, and the daily transactions and interactions you make? When combined, the technologies leading the Fourth Industrial Revolution could have an exponentially transformational effect on our lives. Hence, rather than responding after it happens, we need to be proactive.

We hope that by helping you, the reader, to think creatively about the different possible pathways and developments ahead, this will support and inspire you to create an image of one or more futures that you aspire to live in. An authentic personal vision can serve as a valuable tool in your decision- making—testing each option against it to see if a particular choice would take you towards or away from your preferred future. That vision might look totally different from today; the key is investing the time to understand the developments and choices that could help you take each successive step towards your desired outcome—remembering that the journey itself is normally more valuable and developmental than the destination, and that the vision may evolve as new possibilities unfold.

Rethinking Society

A key theme explored in the book is how society and our organizing structures and norms might be impacted by, and adapt to, the potential changes on the horizon. For more than two centuries, societies have largely organized themselves around the notions of work and learning how to work. The societal goal for almost every human is that we become productive individuals according to predetermined and accepted standards of expected contribution, largely based on our location, social class, and education level. In return, the payoff for the individual is that he or she can earn enough to live, feed, shelter, and clothe their dependents and, maybe one day, reach economic independence.

However, the intrinsic values, ideas, and assumptions upon which these foundational social structures depend are about to get disturbed. We simply don't know and can't yet predict the impact of these exponential technologies on jobs and employment. However, it is fair to assume that there will be significant upheaval—whether most human jobs are automated or there is a dramatic growth of employment opportunities in the industries of tomorrow such as autonomous cars and human augmentation.

Hence, we have to consider the scenarios that differ most from our current assumptions and ask how would we organize society if there were no jobs to do or schools to attend? What would people do if they no longer have to work for a living? What if the foundational societal concepts of careers, leisure time, and retirement disappear? What if these primary aspects of existence vanish amid the Fourth Industrial Revolution?

This transition could be exponentially rapid, confusing, and excruciating, especially if we ignore all the signposts of impending change and fail to act preemptively. Clearly, it is difficult to imagine how societal dynamics and our collective behavior might be disrupted. However, governments can run pilot exercises to explore different possible policy options and their second and third order societal impacts. For example, to counter the risks of mass unemployment, countries such as Canada, Finland, Namibia, and India are experimenting with programs offering a guaranteed or universal basic income (UBI). Already, they are providing valuable insights on implementing different approaches, possible benefits, and unexpected outcomes.

The Future Reinvented – Reimagining Life, Society, and Business sets out to provide examples of how our lives and the functioning of society could be transformed, facilitated by emerging science and technologies. The topics explored range from the near-term trends that could have a longer term impact, to the future of cities, the UK post-Brexit, retirement, education, and the potential to enhance our brains and bodies.

Reimagining Industries and the Future of Business

Perhaps the most obvious impacts of all the changes being discussed in this book will be on the structure and behavior of key industries, and on the purpose, strategy, and organization of business. Nowadays, businesses are the backbone of every contemporary society, which means they sit at the heart of each successive wave of transformational change. As we have witnessed before, enterprises can become vulnerable in unstable times if they are not open to new thinking, experimenting with new ideas, and evolving as quickly as the world around them. Those organizations that fail to ride each wave of innovation runs the risk of drowning due to a lack of a forward-looking culture and mindset.

The new, ever-smarter, and ever-more powerful technologies coming into the workplace can tempt us into choices driven by a desire to maximize cost efficiency and productivity, and thus replacing as many human employees as possible. While this strategy may seem like the obvious solution to today's problems, it might well be the wrong choice for tomorrow.

The risk of automating too far and commoditizing your product or service is very real, as is that of losing the trust of loyal customers because we have so few people left to serve them. The key to survival in the digital age will almost certainly be our ability to use the technology to help unleash human talent. For some time to come, people will still be our best resource to solve wicked problems, serve non-standard customer requests, develop new offerings, and identify new market opportunities.

There is a growing understanding of the major threat total automation represents to the viability of any kind of business. Hence, forward-thinking companies are also investing time and resources to experiment with different organizational forms including cooperative business models and concepts like crowdsourcing and open source platforms. These firms are testing their own physical and mental boundaries and their ability to redefine themselves and what they are capable of.

Many organizations are starting to see that the future is becoming less about assets and balance sheets and more about capability and connection. In the emerging landscape, our true value will increasingly lie in the capacity to implement good ideas quickly, learn from each iteration, refine and repeat. Crucial to such an experimentation-led approach is the nurturing of internal talent.

Models of tomorrow's business are predicated on the engagement of a constantly evolving network, or ecosystem, of external people and agents—partners who the firm supports, encourages, and inspires to help open up and service new markets and opportunities. However, in the constantly evolving model of the networked enterprise, there are also new responsibilities and standards to follow and create. Developing and maintaining real and transparent relationships with all stakeholders will become ever-more important, harder to do, but increasingly profitable and personally enriching.

The Future Reinvented – Reimagining Life, Society, and Business highlights examples of how a range of industry sectors could redefine their role and purpose, harnessing an array of new technologies to deliver fundamentally different product and service propositions. The final section on reimagining business explores how we can place people and ethics at the heart of the agenda, harness emerging technologies to drive growth and transform key business functions.

Chapter Introductions

The Future Reinvented – Reimagining Life, Society, and Business is a collection of the Fast Future's team most recent thinking on upcoming developments and their potential implications for humanity. The book features a total of twenty-three chapters organized into three sections, each focusing on a different level of transformation: life and society, industry, and business. To help you select the topics you most want to read about, we have summarized the content of each chapter below.

Reimagining Life and Society

1. *The Next Future – 40 Key Trends Shaping the Emerging Land-scape* – An overview of forty critical drivers of change across societies that might emerge in 2018, and the possible extent of their impacts over the next five years. Topics encompass lifestyle, politics, people and the workplace, transport, and technology.

2. *Dear Dad: A Letter from a Brighter Future* – A snapshot into an optimistic future where society, politics, environment, economics, and technology interact harmoniously.

3. *Dear Mum: A Letter from Another Future* – A missive from a son to his mother about the struggles of a future filled with technology failing to fulfill its promise, severe economic inequality, ongoing social turmoil, and environmental hardship.

4. *The Future of Work: Retirement in a Post-Work Future* – An overview of the emerging roles for older workers in the Fourth Industrial Revolution, and the possible elimination of retirement.

5. *Intelligent, Connected, and Mobile – Scenarios for Smart, Sustainable, Human Cities* – Scenarios for three smart and very human metropolises of 2030, each highlighting a key driver: data management, artificial intelligence, and green energy.

6. *Britain 2022: The Future Beyond Brexit* – A summary of the results of a flash opinion poll on the future of the UK beyond Brexit, including priorities around social issues, science and technology, and the commercial world.

7. *The Gifts that Keep on Giving: 25 Human Transformations for Your 2030 Christmas Shopping List* – An overview of possible human augmentations, enhancements, and extensions that could become available over the next fifteen years.

8. *Digital Literacy in An Age of Exponential ICT Change* – Arguing the case for raising digital literacy so that we can ensure that information and communications technologies are harnessed to serve society.

Reimagining Industries

Reimagining Business